THEY MET JESUS

Other books by DAVID ALLAN HUBBARD

Is Life Really Worth Living?
What's God Been Doing All This Time?
What's New?
Does the Bible Really Work?
Is the Family Here to Stay?
Psalms for All Seasons
With Bands of Love
The Problem with Prayer Is
How to Face Your Fears
The Holy Spirit in Today's World

THEY MET JESUS

by

David Allan Hubbard

A. J. HOLMAN COMPANY
Division of J. B. Lippincott Company
Philadelphia and New York

The Scripture quotations in this publication are from the Revised
Standard Version of the Bible, copyrighted 1946, 1952, and © 1971
by the Division of Christian Education of the National Council of
the Churches of Christ in the U.S.A. and used by permission.

U.S. Library of Congress Catalog in Publication Data

Hubbard, David Allan.
  They met Jesus.

  Originally presented as a series of radio talks on the international
broadcast the Joyful sound.
1. Bible. N.T.—Biography.   I. The Joyful sound. II. Title.
BS2430.H8   225.9'22 [B]   74-2312
ISBN-0-87981-030-0

Contents

Preface

The four Gospels offer a number of intriguing stories of men and women whose lives were touched by the person of Jesus of Nazareth. Boggled by the unprecedented power of Jesus' presence, the Evangelists chose these stories carefully from among the vast number of episodes they might have recounted. They chose them for a purpose and recounted them without embellishment.

Brief in length and austere in character, these stories have both blessed and baffled their hearers through the centuries. We have been blessed by the picture of the confident, compassionate, reasonable, lordly Christ transforming lives by his word and touch. We have been baffled by the frugality with which the stories are told. We long for more background, more insight.

Why did these persons come to Jesus? How did they feel in his presence? How were their lives different afterward? To get at some answers to these questions, I have tried to read myself into their experiences and to tell their stories in what might have been their own words. To do this takes a bit of license, but I have tried to be as faithful to the Scriptures and as accurate with the setting and culture of New Testament times as I can be.

My friend and colleague Everett F. Harrison, Professor Emeritus of New Testament at Fuller Seminary, has read the manuscript and made a number of helpful suggestions with characteristic kindness. My wife, Ruth, spent many hours improving and typing the text, which was first used in a series of radio talks on the international broadcast, *The Joyful Sound*.

In these pages, we are introduced to men and women who met Jesus, the One who solved their problems and gave their lives meaning. If they speak of themselves, it is only to reveal more of him through whom they found life.

CHAPTER 1

The Man
with the Unclean Spirit

The AUTHORITY of Jesus

And they went into Capernaum; and immediately on the sabbath he entered the synagogue and taught. And they were astonished at his teaching, for he taught them as one who had authority, and not as the scribes. And immediately there was in their synagogue a man with an unclean spirit; and he cried out, "What have you to do with us, Jesus of Nazareth? Have you come to destroy us? I know who you are, the Holy One of God." But Jesus rebuked him, saying, "Be silent, and come out of him!" And the unclean spirit, convulsing him and crying with a loud voice, came out of him. And they were all amazed, so that they questioned among themselves, saying, "What is this? A new teaching! With authority he commands even the unclean spirits, and they obey him." And at once his fame spread everywhere throughout all the surrounding region of Galilee. (Mark 1:21–28.)

M Y FIRST SENSATION was one of total freedom. It was as though I had been tied up for a long time. Not my hands and feet but my spirit. Bondage, confinement, slavery, are the terms that best describe how I felt before. Now I have been set free, like a bird loosed from a cage, like a prisoner whose chains have been broken.

I suppose the suddenness with which it happened contributed to this startling sense of freedom and release. The last thing I had on my mind as I went to the synagogue that sabbath day was that I would be delivered. For years I had gone sabbath by sabbath with my friends at Capernaum to our house of worship. Week after week I had heard the law of Moses read and interpreted. I had watched carefully as the religious leaders of our community unrolled the scrolls that were kept in the sacred ark at the front of the synagogue. I had listened closely as they read from the prophets the passages they thought most appropriate. But the fellowship of the synagogue and the reading of our ancient, holy books brought no relief.

The unclean spirit stayed with me. I was conscious of being under its control night and day. My feelings were not my own. It was as though this devilish thing had invaded my very thoughts and established its headquarters in my mind. It had taken charge of me, and my words were not my own. Neither were my actions. Mind you, at times it would grant me a bit of freedom, a little room to do or say what I wanted. But these times were short-lived. As soon as I began to feel that I was taking charge of my own life again, it would yank on my chains and remind me of how captive I really was.

I tried everything to find permanent relief. Nothing helped. My physician shook his head; he had no remedy for this kind of malady. The rabbis were both puzzled and powerless; their desperate attempt at exorcism had not worked. No medical treatment, no spiritual counsel, brought relief. I was trapped, well enough to take care of my basic needs but not free enough to accomplish anything in life.

You should know that the unclean spirit that possessed me did not lead me into crime or immorality. If it had, I would have been barred from the synagogue and refused access to the spiritual resources of our ancient religion.

No, the demon's attack on me was more emotional. Depression, discouragement and fear were its weapons. I felt worthless most of the time. Confused in my thinking, paralyzed by my fears, I limped and groped my way through life.

Sometimes the demon showed its cruel power by physical torment. Once or twice it wrestled me to the ground and made me roll and writhe. What humiliating experiences! On a few occasions it struck me dumb. I would try to speak, but the words would not come. I would make frantic gestures to try to get my family to understand what I meant. It was horrible.

Then came that unforgettable sabbath when Jesus and his friends visited our synagogue. I had never seen Jesus before. His town, Nazareth, was about a day's journey from my home in Capernaum. When my family made the pilgrimage south to Jerusalem for Passover, we usually followed the shore of the Sea of Galilee. We would travel from the northwest of the lake, following the valley of the Jordan down to Jericho before heading southwest up the hills to Jerusalem. This route made for easier walking because it was less hilly. Besides, it bypassed Samaria and allowed us to avoid contact with those hated Samaritans who had so badly compromised our religion. Going this way, we missed Nazareth by ten or twelve miles since it was in the hills quite a distance to the west, nearer to Cana and Nain.

So I did not recognize Jesus when I saw him. When someone whispered his name I recalled a recent report of his preaching ministry in Galilee. Word was that he was going from town to town talking about a message that he called "the gospel of God." It was a simple and direct message which men summarized by saying, "The time is fulfilled, and the kingdom of God is at hand; repent, and believe in the gospel" (Mark 1:15). I did not really understand what all this meant, at least not until that sabbath in the Capernaum synagogue.

Some of Jesus' friends I did recognize. Simon, whom we later called Peter, and his brother, Andrew, lived in Capernaum. Their reputation as fishermen was well established in the community, and I had done business with them from time to time. Apparently they had recently left their fishing trade to go with Jesus on his preaching tours, but I had heard nothing of that.

The service began as an ordinary sabbath service. First, the *Shema* was read. The *Shema* was like a creed to us. It was the way we confessed our faith in the one true God and acknowledged our commitment to him: "Hear, O Israel: The LORD our God is one LORD; and you shall love the LORD your God with all your heart, and with all your soul, and with all your might" (Deuteronomy 6:4,5). To this were added other passages from Deuteronomy and Numbers which underscored God's commandments and promised blessing to those who keep them: "So you shall remember and do all my commandments, and be holy to your God. I am the LORD your God, who brought you out of the land of Egypt, to be your God: I am the LORD your God." (Numbers 15:40,41.)

This creed meant a lot to me. It told me who my God is and how I fit in his program. It made clear my obligations to him, but it gave me no respite from my problem—that vexing, nagging demon which held my health and my morale in its fiendish clutches.

The synagogue service moved along. It was time for the prayers. Members of the congregation swayed forward and backward in rhythm to the chanting of the prayers and blessings. This was the way we expressed our devotion to God, the intensity of our feelings, as we blessed the name of our God: "Blessed art thou, the Lord our God, and the God of our fathers, the God of Abraham, the God of Isaac, and the God of Jacob: the great, the mighty and terrible God, the most high God who showest mercy and kindness, who createst all things, who rememberest the pious deeds of the patriarchs, and wilt in love bring a redeemer to their children's children for thy name's sake." This was one of our prayers, and I added my own "amen" inwardly to that part about a redeemer, so desperate was I to be set free. Little did I know that in the person of Simon's and Andrew's friend from Nazareth my prayer would be answered.

As the sabbath service proceeded, we listened to the readings from the law and the prophets. Up to this point it had been the usual service, significant, helpful, but not extraordinary. Then the visitor from Nazareth took over. The atmosphere in the synagogue became electric with excitement. The men leaned forward to hear Jesus speak. His was teaching of a sort that neither they nor I had ever heard at Capernaum. Many learned rabbis and scribes had visited our synagogue, but none had been like him.

If I had to put into one word what it was about Jesus' teaching that impressed us and attracted us to him, it would be his *authority*: "for he taught . . . as one who had authority, and not as the scribes" (Mark 1:22). I'm not sure I can explain what I mean, but let me try.

When the scribes interpreted the readings from our great prophets—men like Isaiah, Jeremiah, Amos—they always quoted other scribes or rabbis to back up their interpretations. Their authority was not their own. They were always dependent on the opinions of others. "Rabbi Judah said" or "the scribes of Jerusalem said" was the way they introduced each point. Their authority came from knowing what the teachers who came before them had taught.

With Jesus it was entirely different. He was his own authority. "Truly, truly, I say to you" was the way he began. Why, it was as though the prophets themselves were speaking. I had often wondered what it would have been like to have been present when Isaiah made his great speeches to King Ahaz or when Amos stood before the wealthy leaders of Samaria and exposed their crimes. Now I knew. With the very authority of God, this man from Nazareth opened up the meaning of the Scriptures clearly, accurately, powerfully.

And then it happened. The unclean spirit began to stir within. Apparently it was moved by Jesus' authority too. In a flash it began to speak through me. Almost in panic my voice rang out: "What have you to do with us, Jesus of Nazareth? Have you come to destroy us? I know who you are, the Holy One of God." (Mark 1:24.)

The demon was wiser than the rest of us. We were puzzled at the astonishing authority garbed in carpenter's clothes, the uncanny insight expressed with the familiar accents of Galilee. But the demon knew that it was in the Messiah's presence, and that the Messiah's presence spelled doom for it and all its hellish comrades. That's why it panicked. That's why it cried out from within me.

Then Jesus took charge. He had demonstrated his authority in his teaching. Now he dramatized it in his actions. "Be silent, and come out of him!" he commanded. The demon knew it had to obey. It had met its master and more.

But what a struggle it put up—almost like a fight to the death. With loud angry cries it clung to me, wrenching and twisting me. It threw me to the synagogue floor before the amazed stares of my fellow worshipers. Then, as swiftly as it had begun, the struggle was over. Jesus had won. My enemy had vanished.

The synagogue was a hubbub of exclamations: " 'What is this? A new teaching! With authority he commands even the unclean spirits, and they obey him.' " (Mark 1:27.) *With authority*, was the phrase that popped up again and again, and what a welcome phrase it was to me! All those years I had been held in chains, fettered, tethered and tied. Then I met One with authority who took charge and set me free. The forces of hell itself were not strong enough to defy him.

That's why reports of his authority swept the countryside like a storm. Other people, including a few of my friends and relatives, had similar experiences with him.

Thirty years have come and gone since that sabbath, that dramatic turning point in my life, that pivotal episode which Jesus' disciples have talked and written about. Freedom has been my joy every day throughout this time. More than ever I realize how significant that event was. In a crucial contest of authority Christ won. He outranks every other power, whether human or diabolical. Mine was a test case, and Jesus won. And he has been winning ever since.

CHAPTER 2

Simon Peter's
Mother-in-Law

The CONSIDERATION of Jesus

And immediately he left the synagogue, and entered the house of Simon and Andrew, with James and John. Now Simon's mother-in-law lay sick with a fever, and immediately they told him of her. And he came and took her by the hand and lifted her up, and the fever left her; and she served them.

That evening, at sundown, they brought to him all who were sick or possessed with demons. And the whole city was gathered together about the door. And he healed many who were sick with various diseases, and cast out many demons; and he would not permit the demons to speak, because they knew him. (Mark 1:29-34.)

I T WAS ONE of the worst days of my life. I was sick and I was frustrated. We had looked forward to that sabbath, my daughter and I. We knew that Simon and Andrew would be with us for dinner. And we knew that with them they would bring Jesus, the prophet from Nazareth whom they had just begun to follow.

Simon, my daughter's husband, had asked us to prepare a special meal for his special guest. All day Friday we had worked. By sundown, when the sabbath began and all work had to cease, we were ready. The round, flat loaves of bread had been baked, and they were just the right size and texture to break in pieces and to dip in the rich sauce that was part of our main dish. We had even used wheat flour this time instead of barley, which was cheaper and, for this reason, was the staple of our daily diet.

The vegetables were prepared, and for an added treat we had roasted part of a young goat. Pickled olives we would serve, and our special sauce, a blend of dates, raisins, figs and vinegar. Usually we saved it for Passover, but this was a special occasion.

As we worked on the meal, mixing the dough, cleaning the vegetables, preparing the spices—mint, cummin, mustard—we talked about this man Jesus, with whom Simon and Andrew had cast their lots. What a man he must be to get these two brothers to follow him! Born for fishing they were, with broad backs for lifting their catches, tough hands for handling their nets and brave spirits to cope with wind and wave. Fishing was not just their trade; it was their life.

Now they had left it to follow him. You can imagine my daughter's anxiety when Simon told her what he and Andrew had decided. She didn't know what to think. With tears she pleaded with him not to be rash, to weigh the implications of his decision for her and the whole family. But the big fisherman's mind was made up. He could hardly explain why. "I feel called to do this" was the way he put it. "God has spoken to me. He is doing a new thing in our land, and I must be part of it."

No way to argue with convictions like those. So we tried to make the best of his commitment and to prepare ourselves for better or worse. These were some of the things we chatted about, my daughter and I, as we prepared for the big sabbath meal. I tried to reassure her that all would be well, that it was her duty to support and encourage her man in his new calling. But, I confess, inwardly I was almost as uncertain as she was.

Naturally we both looked forward to meeting Jesus. Simon's description of him—his love, his power, his wisdom—had been unbelievable. Our curiosity was at a peak, especially since the whole direction of our lives was being changed by a man we had not yet met.

Finally the dinner was prepared, and the table was set. Shaped like a horseshoe, the table was only a couple of feet high. Around it were low couches where Simon, Andrew and their friends would recline. Resting on their left forearms, they would have their right hands free to take that good wheat bread we had just baked and dip it like a spoon in our tasty sauces and gravies. Those fishermen could eat, and we were ready for them.

I had planned to serve them and eat later. It's hard being up and down bringing more food and drink from the kitchen, so I would rather help our guests enjoy their dinner and their intimate conversation than eat with them. Speaking of conversation, I must admit that I had hoped to overhear as much as possible, if only to see if Simon had been exaggerating in his accounts of the charm and prowess of his friend from Nazareth.

Bone tired from the long day of cooking and cleaning, I went to bed early on Friday night, not long after sundown. My sleep was fitful, and at first I thought I was just overly tired from my day's work and excited about the sabbath's activities. But in the middle of the night it hit me—I was ill, feverishly ill. I tossed on my low cot, alternately throwing off the covers as the fever burned and tucking them in around me as the chills shook me. I tried to be as quiet as possible, knowing that my daughter was as tired as I was. Softly I lifted my voice to God for help, but the fever raged on.

At dawn the rest of the family began to stir, but the fever had glued me to my bed. My pillow was soaked with perspiration, and my spirits were just as soggy. I knew that there was no way that I could participate in the events of the day. My strength was gone, and with it went my hopes of helping and serving on the greatest day our household had yet seen. My daughter came in to see why I had not gotten up. She tried to comfort me some as she sponged my face and arms with cool water, but it did little good.

As the day wore on I dozed a little, drifting in and out of reality, almost delirious at times. I woke to the sound of voices. My daughter's voice I could distinguish, but the others I did not recognize. They were high and boyish and not like the rich, deep tones of Simon or Andrew.

I did not have long to wait to find out who the visitors were. My daughter came bursting into the room, a bundle of excitement. "The neighbor boys stopped by on their way home from the synagogue." Her words were flying at a leopard's pace. "You won't believe what happened. Jesus began to teach after the reading from the prophets. Then that man who has an unclean spirit—you know who I mean, the man who lives on the other side of town—stood up in the synagogue and began to tell Jesus to leave him alone. He even called Jesus 'the Holy One of God,' as though he knew that Jesus was our Messiah."

My daughter hardly paused for breath. "Then Jesus took charge. He rebuked the demon and commanded it to come out of the man. The synagogue was in an uproar. The poor man was in convulsions, writhing on the floor, with the synagogue leaders standing over him watching. Then, suddenly, there was peace. The demon was gone and the man was free. Talk about authority! Now I know what Simon meant when he said that there was no way he could say no to Jesus' call."

My daughter had barely finished her whirlwind description of the episode in the synagogue when we heard voices in the courtyard and knew that our men were home. She rushed to meet them, not only to wash their feet, but to hear firsthand what Jesus had done.

I was wide awake now and I began to muse. Why was I so weak? I who scarcely knew a day of sickness in my life was flat on my back on what might have been one of the greatest days I had ever known. But I also mused about the power of Jesus. I knew that man with the unclean spirit and I had witnessed his hysterical conduct, his absurd speech, his fits of frenzy. Yet a word from Jesus set him free.

I could almost believe this, because I had seen what Jesus' words had done to Simon. That blustery son-in-law of mine had suddenly found new purpose. He had a sense of mission that was more important to him than his fishing, something I never thought could happen.

Not that he was cruel or unkind before. He certainly has been good to me since my husband died. In fact it was he who bore the terrible news to me the evening of the great storm. My husband's boat had been swamped, and the other boats were fighting to stay afloat. Then the rudder on my husband's boat snapped like a twig between strong fingers and he was swept overboard. That was it.

Since that sad night, Simon has treated me like his own mother. His home has been my home. What he has I have shared in. He has always been a good man, although he was not famous for his patience. My daughter used to chide him by asking why he could be so patient searching at night for fish in the Sea of Galilee, and so impatient waiting for her to prepare his meals on shore in Capernaum.

But in these last few weeks since he met Jesus, Simon has changed. It's not just that his gruffness has mellowed some. It's that his whole view of life has been transformed. He talks of God's kingdom which Jesus is bringing; he claims that people everywhere should repent; he even calls himself a "fisher of men."

In the midst of my musing they came into my room—Simon, my daughter and Jesus. Here he was in my room and by my side, the one who had given orders to demons and who had set a strong fisherman on a different course. Almost without a word, he reached down and took me by the arm and lifted me out of the cot which had been my prison through a hot night and a dismal day. His touch was strong and gentle; his gaze was steady and compassionate; his look was gracious and confident. As I stood, the fever left. A strength, as though from heaven, surged through my body. That frightful combination of frailty and frustration had fled. I tarried a moment to thank the King of the universe for answering my prayer and then I joined my daughter in the kitchen. Together we served our men and their guests.

Authority is what Jesus had demonstrated in the synagogue that day, authority in his teaching and authority in his control of the evil spirit. And I certainly sensed that same authority. The fever had no chance when he entered the room.

But it was his consideration more than his authority that I remember as I look back on the day when his cool touch drove fear and fever out of my troubled frame. I was a stranger to him, yet he seemed to sense my discouragement and hurried to lift it. I was a woman and an in-law, yet before he did anything else in our home, he came to help me.

My plight, my pain, my sense of disappointment, my desire to serve, to listen and to learn—all these he seemed to understand. His eyes shone with consideration; his touch radiated it. He seemed consumed with me and my needs at that moment. Shut out were the noise and clamor of the synagogue. He directed his whole attention and he focused his full power on me and my problem. I was refreshed, relaxed, ready to serve as though I had just awakened from a peaceful sleep.

Placed beside the great miracles that Jesus worked in his three years of public ministry, most of which Simon witnessed and reported to my daughter and me, what happened to me may not seem sensational. It was one of many magnificent acts that took place on that same day. For when the sabbath ended at sundown, "they brought to him all who were sick or possessed with demons. And the whole city was gathered together about the door. And he healed many who were sick with various diseases, and cast out many demons." (Mark 1: 32–34.)

What a day! What power, what authority, and especially what consideration! Let others remember him as they will; I will always hold in mind the gentle touch, the considerate look. Think of it. He did this for me, a woman, and a mother-in-law at that! No wonder Simon said that in Jesus a new day had dawned.

CHAPTER 3

The Man Who Lived Among the Tombs in Gerasa

The POWER of Jesus

They came to the other side of the sea, to the country of the Gerasenes. And when he had come out of the boat, there met him out of the tombs a man with an unclean spirit, who lived among the tombs; and no one could bind him any more, even with a chain; for he had often been bound with fetters and chains, but the chains he wrenched apart, and the fetters he broke in pieces; and no one had the strength to subdue him. Night and day among the tombs and on the mountains he was always crying out, and bruising himself with stones. And when he saw Jesus from afar, he ran and worshiped him; and crying out with a loud voice, he said, "What have you to do with me, Jesus, Son of the Most High God? I adjure you by God, do not torment me." For he had said to him, "Come out of the man, you unclean spirit!" And Jesus asked him, "What is your name?" He replied, "My name is Legion; for we are many." And he begged him eagerly not to send them out of the country. Now a great herd of swine was feeding there on the hillside; and they begged him, "Send us to the swine, let us enter them." So he gave them leave. And the unclean spirits came out, and entered the swine; and the herd, numbering about two thousand, rushed down the steep bank into the sea, and were drowned in the sea.

The herdsmen fled, and told it in the city and in the country. And people came to see what it was that had happened. And they came to Jesus, and saw the demoniac sitting there, clothed and in his right mind, the man who had had the legion; and they were afraid. And those who had seen it told what had happened to the demoniac and to the swine. And they began to beg Jesus to depart from their neighborhood. And as he was getting into the boat, the man who had been possessed with demons begged him that he might be with him. But he refused, and said to him, "Go home to your friends, and tell them how much the Lord has done for you, and how he has had mercy on you." And he went away and began to proclaim in the Decapolis how much Jesus had done for him; and all men marveled. (Mark 5:1–20.)

WOULD YOU BELIEVE that I once lived among these tombs? These cliffs, with their caves like honeycombs, were my home. I was living among the dead in those days. When I needed shelter I would crawl into a tomb and either crouch in the round opening or huddle on the low shelf where the body had been laid.

How did I move the large checkerlike stones which rolled in the groove before the doorway? Well, you may not believe it, but I had superhuman strength in those days. The large, well-cut stones that guarded the graves of the rich I could put my shoulder to and shove aside. The smaller stones that the poorer people piled up to protect the tombs of their loved ones I could lift high above my head and send crashing down the cliffs to the plains below.

You can imagine how terrified the people were who had to bury their dead. How could there be proper mourning for a member of the family with a madman raging and roaring through the burial site? The women who came out to embalm the bodies with spices and to bind them with the strong linen wrappings were craven with fear. It was bad enough to have to lay aside a loved one, to wrap the cold, stiff limbs, to gaze lovingly at a face that no longer returned the gaze; but to do all this to the accompaniment of a frenzied, naked maniac must have been insufferable.

The situation was so bad at times that groups of people from the city where I used to live came to bind me. But the chains they carried were to no avail; I snapped them like thread. And the linen cords I broke like string. Ten men could not hold me down even if they could catch me, which they rarely could because I knew the terrain like the back of my hand. Its caves and stones, its humps and hollows, offered so many hiding places that I could disappear like a black cat on a dark night.

These tombs on this steep hillside were my home. Not that my family wanted it that way. But what could they do? I was strong; I was wild. My brothers did their best to persuade me to return—at first, that is. Then they realized that I was driven by powers greater than my own or theirs.

When I had lived in the city with my family, I had to be kept under guard, even chained at times. But that did no good when the demons raged within me. Under their wicked power, I would tear away the chains, rip off my clothes and race off to some deserted spot like these tombs.

I guess they were symbolic, the tombs. I was more dead than alive—my powers of reason gone, my family and friends ashamed. As I look back I see that I really wanted to die. In fact I deliberately used to cut and bruise myself with stones. What a sight I must have been, stark naked, scampering among the graves, frantically racing up the mountainside, shrieking and wailing like some strange animal.

Then that day came, and through the heat haze I saw the boat land. Nothing special about that, I suppose. I often watched the small boats beach themselves on the shoreline. It was the southeast corner of the Sea of Galilee, and although it was not as busy, perhaps, as some parts of the lake, there were plenty of boats. If the fishermen or other travelers used to venture too far up the hillside toward my cemetery home, I would let out one of my wild shrieks and send a stone or two crashing down toward them.

But that day was different. Somehow I was fascinated by the men who beached their boat and began the long, twisting climb up the mountainside. I watched them wending their way, step by step, pausing for breath and for glimpses of the lake they knew so well. One man in particular caught my eye. Perhaps it was partly his stature and bearing; partly it was because he was the obvious leader of the group. Chatting now with some of his men and now with others, he continued to climb. And I continued to watch. The poise he manifested, the grace of his gestures, his gentle firmness—all these drew me to him as the strong bulls of Bashan were drawn to their watering holes. When I could see him closer and hear his voice, my first impressions were confirmed. No one like him had ever walked my way before.

Then he was at the top of the cliff, and, without thinking, I ran to him and fell flat on my face before him as though to worship him. Although I did not know his name, I heard myself crying out with a loud voice: "What have you to do with me, Jesus, Son of the Most High God? I adjure you by God, do not torment me." (Mark 5:7.)

Almost before I realized what was going on, this man sized up the situation perfectly. My unkempt condition, my raw nakedness, my wild look and my perception of who he was all combined to tell him that I was demon possessed. My conduct, my habits, my words, were not my own.

And before Jesus spoke to me he spoke to the demon that haunted me and commanded it to come out. I can't describe the turmoil of that moment. The powerful words of Jesus, his forceful gesture and his fixed gaze were met with the fiercest opposition by the spirit within me. The demon even invoked the name of God in his desperate plea to be let alone: "I adjure you by God, do not torment me."

The struggle was brief. Jesus' power began to assert itself, a power that could belong only to the Son of the Most High God, as the demon had called him. Jesus showed how secure he was, how confident of his power, as he continued to speak to the demon: "What is your name?" It was as though he wanted to make his command as direct and specific as possible by calling the demon by name.

I'll never forget the demon's reply: "My name is Legion; for we are many" (Mark 5:9). Those few words explained my years of torture. This was no single demon that drove me wild, stripped me of my reason and my clothes, infused me with the might of a centurion's guard. This was a host of demons, a company of spirits, a whole cadre of Satan's servants—a legion of them.

I had not merely been harassed by an unclean spirit, one of Satan's scouts sent to spy out the land, I had been invaded by an army. Legion was their name; for they were many. Never since that day have I seen the Roman soldiers who occupy our land without thinking of that other invasion army. When I hear the rhythmic slap of sandals on stone as the soldiers march along the Roman roads which bind our cities together,

I remember that other legion. Especially when I walk that great road to Gerasa do I remember. That road too broad for dust to obscure, too firm for rain to destroy, leads to the great Roman garrison that guards the territory between the winding Jordan and the savage desert. The Roman legion is there in force in Gerasa, but my legion is gone.

The power in Jesus did them in. And in an incredible way. The gentile herdsmen who settled in this territory after the time of Alexander the Great used to raise pigs here. You can imagine how distasteful this was to the Jews who lived here. Pigs were declared unclean in their law. But more than that, about two hundred years ago Antiochus Epiphanes, one of the Syrian rulers who inherited this part of the world when Alexander's empire was broken up, actually sacrificed a pig in the temple at Jerusalem. This the Jews never forgot. The "abomination of desolation," they called it. It made the temple unfit for use until it could be thoroughly cleansed and purified with elaborate ceremony.

Anyway, the gentile herdsmen used to pasture their swine on the tops of these cliffs near the old cemetery where I once lived. For reasons that I have never quite understood, the demons wanted to be sent into the swine. I guess they did not wish to return to hell where they belonged. Jesus granted their wish. And when they were driven out of me by the power of his command, they rushed into the swine and sent them plunging over the precipice into the sea.

Actually the herdsmen were the first to bear the news to my family and friends. Strange irony this, that gentile swine-herders, who cared nothing about God's promises of a Messiah, should become heralds of such good tidings.

Fear was the first reaction of the people who came to test

the reports with their own eyes—fear at seeing me sitting, not raging; clothed, not naked; and in my right mind, not beside myself with frenzy. The powerful hand of God had been at work, and fear was the people's response.

As for me, I suppose I shared that sense of fear. After all, I had experienced that awesome power firsthand. But my fear was different from theirs. They wanted to get rid of Jesus, to send him away, to forget what had happened. Their pattern of life had been ruffled, to say the least. Their livelihood, dependent as they were on the pigs, had been put in jeopardy. They had been threatened by power that was too much for them. Their way of dealing with it and with the fear that it sparked was to beg Jesus to leave and never to return.

But what had happened had a different effect on me. I was afraid, of course, afraid that the legion might march back into my life and raise their cruel flag of conquest once again. I walked down the hillside with Jesus. I even tried to get into the boat with him. His friends practically had to tear him away, so eager was I to go with him. Then he explained why I had to stay: "Go home to your friends, and tell them how much the Lord has done for you, and how he has had mercy on you" (Mark 5:19).

I stood and watched and waved until the boat was a small dot on the blue lake. Then I ran up the hillside as the tiny craft disappeared in the evening dusk.

With fear and trembling I went about my mission in the area where the Greeks and Romans had established ten cities —the Decapolis, we called them. My fear gave way to joy as men and women who had known me before, and even total strangers, marveled at the news of my rescue.

I come back to these tombs from time to time to reflect on

Jesus and what he did for me. Over the months and years I have heard much about his wisdom, his love, his authority, his concern. But it will always be his power to which I bear witness. His power took me from the tombs and put me on the highroads of life. His power conquered a whole legion and sent them rattled and scattered in defeat. His power used gentile herdsmen and their unclean swine for his purposes. And his power gave meaning to a hopeless maniac.

I like to come back to these tombs to remember. And to give thanks.

CHAPTER 4

Jairus, the Ruler Whose Daughter Died

The CONFIDENCE of Jesus

And when Jesus had crossed again in the boat to the other side, a great crowd gathered about him; and he was beside the sea. Then came one of the rulers of the synagogue, Jairus by name; and seeing him, he fell at his feet, and besought him, saying, "My little daughter is at the point of death. Come and lay your hands on her, so that she may be made well, and live." And he went with him.

And a great crowd followed him and thronged about him. And there was a woman who had had a flow of blood for twelve years, and who had suffered much under many physicians, and had spent all that she had, and was no better but rather grew worse. She had heard the reports about Jesus, and came up behind him in the crowd and touched his garment. For she said, "If I touch even his garments, I shall be made well." And immediately the hemorrhage ceased; and she felt in her body that she was healed of her disease. And Jesus, perceiving in himself that power had gone forth from him, immediately turned about in the crowd, and said, "Who touched my garments?" And his disciples said to him, "You see the crowd pressing around you, and yet you say, 'Who touched me?' " And he looked around to see who had done it. But the woman, knowing what had been done to her, came in fear and trembling and fell down before him, and told him the whole truth. And he said to her, "Daughter, your faith has made you well; go in peace, and be healed of your disease."

While he was still speaking, there came from the ruler's house some who said, "Your daughter is dead. Why trouble the Teacher any further?" But ignoring what they said, Jesus said to the ruler of the synagogue, "Do not fear, only believe." And he allowed no one to follow him except Peter and James and John the brother of James. When they came to the house of the ruler of the synagogue, he saw a tumult, and people weeping and wailing loudly. And when he had entered, he said to them, "Why do you make a tumult and weep? The child is not dead but sleeping." And they laughed at him. But he put them all outside, and took the child's father and mother and those who were with him, and went in where the child was. Taking her by the hand he said to her, "Talitha cumi"; which means, "Little girl, I say to you, arise." And immediately the girl got up and walked; for she was twelve years old. And immediately they were overcome with amazement. And he strictly charged them that no one should know this, and told them to give her something to eat. (Mark 5:21–43.)

I HAD NEVER DONE anything like that before. But in my desperation I found myself lying on my face before Jesus. Never in my life had I shown such deference to another man.

In fact, through the years I had grown much more accustomed to receiving respect than to showing it. Especially since the time I became ruler of the synagogue, men have shown their regard for me and my position. When I enter the marketplace, the younger men make room for me and wait for me to speak first. Even the elders of Capernaum pay heed to my words.

As ruler of the synagogue I am responsible for the administration and management of the various services. It is I who select the men who read the passages from the law and the prophets. It is I who give permission for visitors to speak, especially those who wish to make comments on the Scripture lessons. Now that I think of it, this was the way I first met Jesus. It was that sabbath when he came to the synagogue at Capernaum with Peter and Andrew and asked to say a few words.

Teaching like that I had never heard—authority beyond that of any scribe or rabbi I had ever met; and I suppose that I knew most of the learned men of the land. Then, when he capped the authority of his teaching by sending an unclean spirit whimpering away in defeat like a whipped dog, I knew that someone extraordinary had come on the scene.

Now I found myself flat on my face before him. More desperate than a beggar, I implored him to come to the aid of my family. Nor was I ashamed to prostrate myself before him. I was at the end of my rope. All our efforts to help my little daughter recover from her illness had failed. The time-honored remedies—potions that we gave her to drink and ointments that we applied to her body—had failed and left her weaker. The best physicians of Capernaum had attended her day and night. Perplexed, they watched her health deteriorate before their eyes.

All that I had I would have exchanged to see color surge through her pallid cheeks. Wealth, prominence, recognition, power, fade into insignificance at such moments. The issues of life and death cause all other circumstances to pale.

Then I heard that Jesus and his men had just returned from a trip to the southern end of the lake near Gadara, and I set out to look for him. He was not hard to find. Those were his days of great popularity. Follow the crowds and find that they lead to Jesus. That's what I did.

Not even pausing to greet my friends or to return the salutations of those who recognized me, I pushed through the throng to Jesus' side. Impulsively I dropped to my knees and then fell forward on my face at his feet. My words came in brief, sharp gasps: "My little daughter is at the point of death." I almost choked on the word. Then I steeled myself and pushed ahead:

"Come and lay your hands on her, so that she may be made well, and live" (Mark 5:23).

"And live"—how good those words sounded. Almost too good to be true. Did I dare hope? Would he come? What would he do if he did come?

Two memories gave me heart to put my request to him. The first I have already mentioned—the memory of Jesus' mighty authority in action, casting out the unclean spirit from the man in the synagogue. And there was the equally impressive episode when Jesus healed the centurion's servant. In that case Jesus had not even needed to be present. Here were two men I knew in our own town, one possessed of a demon, the other a Roman officer. If Jesus responded to their needs, would he not respond to mine?

And respond he did, quicker than I could have hoped for. He helped me to my feet, and we were on the way to my house. As we walked, surrounded by the crowd that followed spontaneously, I asked myself what it was about Jesus that impressed me. His bearing? His poise? His composure? His confidence? I think that's it—his confidence.

Without hesitation he moved to help me. He asked me no questions about my daughter's symptoms. He offered no excuse as to why he might not be able to help her. He just came with me—calm, quiet, confident.

We walked as fast as we could, given the size of the crowds. Wherever possible I worked my way through the bunches of people who were struggling to get a look at Jesus, and I took him by the arm to lead him through behind me.

All at once I noticed that he had stopped in his tracks and was bent over, talking to a woman who had fallen at his feet. You can guess how impatient I was. My daughter was at the point of death, yet Jesus stopped to chat with a woman. I pressed closer to them, to overhear the conversation and to see if I dared urge Jesus to move on.

As I listened, the woman began fearfully and hesitantly to tell her whole story. For twelve years she had been plagued with constant hemorrhaging. Her strength had been drained; her morale had been destroyed; her funds had been exhausted; her friendships had been dissolved. She was a total wreck.

Physicians had performed costly experiments on her, and she had grown worse. Priests and rabbis shunned her because her constant bleeding made her unclean according to the law of Moses. Anyone who touched her during this condition had to undergo special ceremonies of purification. My heart went out to her as she told her story, yet my own daughter was still at the point of death.

Ashamed of the nature of her illness and chagrined to talk about it with a man, the woman had slipped up behind Jesus to try to touch him. She had heard of the power of his touch on others, and she thought that if she touched *him*, his power might work the same way.

Even in the huge crowd with everyone bumping and pushing, Jesus felt her touch. She had grabbed the tassel of his cloak as it hung over his shoulder and down his back. All of us Jews wore an overgarment that had tassels at the four corners, as the Lord had commanded Moses: "Speak to the people of Israel, and bid them to make tassels on the corners of their garments throughout their generations, and to put upon the tassel of each corner a cord of blue; and it shall be to you a tassel to look upon and remember all the commandments of the LORD, to do them . . ." (Numbers 15:38,39). This tassel, with its special message of obedience to God, she clutched for a brief moment in the hope that through it she could drain power from Jesus. And she did. She felt it immediately. The flow of blood stopped, and she was well.

With tender patience Jesus heard her story. His words to her were simple and powerful: "Daughter, your faith has made you well; go in peace, and be healed of your disease" (Mark 5:34). The word "daughter" gave me a start. I had become so engrossed in the woman's tragic story that for a moment my own heaviness had lifted.

Then I thought again of my daughter, of the great invest-ment of love and care I had in her, of the years during which my wife and I had nurtured her like a tender plant, guarded her like a gentle lamb, rejoiced in her as in a pearl beyond price.

I regretted the delay in our journey, yet I found my faith strengthened as Jesus brought the conversation to a close. Again his quiet confidence struck me. He had assured her of her healing without any inquiry or examination. A touch of his tassel, and she was well.

Suddenly, as I pondered these things, some of my servants came bursting into the packed throng like wolves into a flock of sheep. They surrounded me, and their spokesman blurted out the dreaded words: "Your daughter is dead. Why trouble the Teacher any further?" (Mark 5:35.) The words were quite unnecessary. I could read the message in the look of their faces—drawn, dark, dismal.

The worst had happened. In the midst of the joy of this woman's healing came the news of my daughter's death. I looked at Jesus. What would his response be now?

It was as though he had not heard the grim report. His quiet confidence was unruffled. Amid the joyful celebration of a

healing and the doleful news of a death, Jesus remained his
calm, composed, controlled self: "Do not fear, only believe"
(Mark 5:36). He knew what I felt and what I needed better
than I. Ruler of the synagogue or not, prominent citizen of
Capernaum or not, I put myself completely in his hands. He
had given me good grounds to believe. Now I had to do just
that.

We found the courtyard of my house in an uproar. Even
before we turned off the main street we could hear it: weeping,
wailing, the sad sounds of the mourning flutes, the loud
howls of the professional lamenters. The confusion was short-
lived when Jesus took charge: "Why do you make a tumult
and weep? The child is not dead but sleeping." (Mark 5:39.)

Their answer was laughter—mocking laughter. My wife and
her servants had heard the girl's last sigh. They had seen her
breathing stop. They had stared into glassy eyes and held a
mirror to her mouth and nose. No life, no breath, no sound.
The servants and the mourners laughed; taut and nervous
they were, so they laughed. Jesus ran them out of the courtyard. That authority which before my eyes had sent a demon
scurrying made them scatter like frightened birds.

Then Jesus took us inside—my wife and me, Peter, James
and John, the men closest to him. There was no ritual, no
spell, no ceremony. There was no inquiry, no investigation,
no examination. Jesus simply took my daughter by the hand
and said, "Child, arise." As easily as if she had been wakened
from an afternoon nap, she stood up and walked.

The sight and smell of death gave way to the blush and
fragrance of life. Color painted her cheeks; light sparked from
her eyes; her flesh glowed with warmth. Beside ourselves with

amazement and joy, my wife and I embraced each other and then our daughter, then Jesus and then his men.

With the same quiet confidence, Jesus told us to give her something to eat. The victory was complete. She was back to normal, ready to eat.

I've relived these scenes a thousand times, and always one picture looms large: the confident Jesus, confident without brashness, confident yet compassionate. A nameless woman sick for twelve years. The twelve-year-old daughter of a synagogue ruler. Jesus in full control of a defiling disease and death itself.

Flat on my face I had found myself begging for his help. A thousand times since, I have reenacted those events, rehearsed those conversations. My reaction is always the same. Flat on my face. Then, it was to beg. Now, it is to give thanks —to give thanks for the *confidence* of Christ.

CHAPTER 5

The Persistent Gentile Woman from Phoenicia

The REASONABLENESS of Jesus

And Jesus went away from there and withdrew to the district of Tyre and Sidon. And behold, a Canaanite woman from that region came out and cried, "Have mercy on me, O Lord, Son of David; my daughter is severely possessed by a demon." But he did not answer her a word. And his disciples came and begged him, saying, "Send her away, for she is crying after us." He answered, "I was sent only to the lost sheep of the house of Israel." But she came and knelt before him, saying, "Lord, help me." And he answered, "It is not fair to take the children's bread and throw it to the dogs." She said, "Yes, Lord, yet even the dogs eat the crumbs that fall from their master's table." Then Jesus answered her, "O woman, great is your faith! Be it done for you as you desire." And her daughter was healed instantly. (Matthew 15: 21–28.)

I HAD TRIED everything I knew, and my daughter's case was still hopeless. The priests at the temple near my home had applied all their techniques for getting rid of demons, but my daughter was still possessed.

I can still hear the chanting of their ancient incantations:

> "Be off! Be off! Depart! Depart!
> Your wickedness like smoke rises heavenward!
> By the life of the sun-god, the mighty, verily
>   be ye exorcized!"

And the various ceremonies they went through! One time the priests made a fire and placed on the embers the heart and liver of a fish. They hoped the demon would smell the stench and flee, never to return. Once they even resorted to the ancient Canaanite practice of sympathetic magic. They took a lump of clay and molded it in a shape they said resembled the figure of the evil spirit. After a series of magical incantations and mystical jabberings, they broke the clay figurine. This act of magic was supposed to destroy the demon.

Nothing worked; not their chanting incantations, not their smoking fish livers, not their ancient magic. They called on all the gods they knew. They called on the Greek gods which our people had learned about after the invasions of Alexander, when Hellenistic culture and the Greek language, which I speak, were brought to our shores. They called on our ancient Canaanite gods which we had worshiped in Phoenicia throughout the centuries of our history: gods like Malik, our king god; Baal, god of fertility; and the great goddess Anat, Baal's wife. They called on the names of the Egyptian gods which we had come to know in our trading ventures with Egypt: gods like Osiris and his wife, Isis. They had even called on the Roman gods Juno and Jupiter, of whom we had learned from the Roman officials and soldiers who had occupied our coastal plain for a hundred years or so.

But nothing worked. The only results were increasing frustration for my daughter, who found no peace or relief, and an increasing burden for me, who not only had to care for her but had to pay the priests for these expensive treatments.

Then reports of a miracle worker began to filter over the hills from Galilee to the Mediterranean shores where we made our home in the region dominated by our two great seaports, Tyre and Sidon. Sailors and traders, my ancestors were. They dyed the purple cloth that was in demand in Greece and Asia. They hauled the huge cedars from the mountains of Lebanon, the most sought-after timber in the Middle East, and shipped them to far-off ports. Clear to Carthage on the coast of Africa they sailed and settled, the finest sailors and merchants of our world.

But it was not to our illustrious past that I could look for help. I had done that through my priests, and discouragement was my reward. These new reports turned my eyes away from the coasts of Tyre and Sidon, away from our religion with its mixture of Canaanite, Egyptian, Greek and Roman beliefs, to the God of Israel and one whom some called David's son.

The reports that drifted over the hills were hard to believe. A young girl, the daughter of a religious official in Capernaum, was brought back from the dead by a word and a touch from this Son of David, Jesus by name. And always with the reports of healing were accounts of deliverance from demon power.

It was hard for me to credit these accounts at first. That Galilean world over the hills was not far. Traders and their caravans could make the trip in a couple of days. But it seemed a lot farther away than that. It was a different world. A world where the names of our gods were swearwords, where our idols and religious rites were blasphemy, where the seafoods and swine that we ate were an abomination. Not that we thought much about their religion either. It seemed harsh and rigid to us, with its countless rules and regulations about diet, dress, feast, fast and sabbaths. Those sabbaths would have been intolerable to us: no travel, no work, no nothing!

What irritated us most and put an insurmountable barrier between us and the Jewish people was their insufferable pride. You would think the world was created for them, and only they had a right to it. Although backward in their culture and far less sophisticated in the Greek customs and learning which Alexander's troops had brought, they somehow thought they knew it all, especially when it came to religion. I'll tell you now, their religion held no appeal for me, but the reports of the wonders wrought by Jesus did.

And that's why I set out to find him. Rumors were rampant

that he had left Galilee to hide for a while. His controversies with the religious leaders had apparently broken into open conflict. His cousin and close associate, John the Baptist, had been cruelly put to death at Herod's birthday party. Pressure against Jesus was mounting, and he chose to withdraw for a season.

My heart leaped within me when I heard that he had come to the edge of our territory and was staying in a nearby town. When I found him in the marketplace, I was nearly out of my mind with excitement: "Have mercy on me, O Lord, Son of David; my daughter is severely possessed by a demon" (Matthew 15:22). The words poured from my lips as though pumped out by my pounding heart. And I waited for Jesus' reply.

It was the shock of my life. All the reports from Galilee, and especially Capernaum, had sounded a common theme: the compassion, the understanding, the reasonableness of Jesus. He was sensitive to people's hurts; he was open to their needs. On these reports my hope was built. What was Jesus' response to me and my plea? Silence. Stony silence, harsh and hard like the rocky coasts of my country. No answer at all would he give me.

Finally his disciples broke the silence with a grim request: "Send her away, for she is crying after us" (Matthew 15:23). True, I had pressed them to take me to Jesus. When they refused, I followed them to find out where he was staying.

When Jesus finally spoke, as if to explain his silence, it did not really help: "I was sent only to the lost sheep of the house of Israel"(Matthew 15:24).

My mind was flooded with possible rejoinders. What about all those reports of compassion and understanding? Were they lies? How can you be so cruel? You have the power, yet you refuse to help! If I had let go, my tongue would have galloped in all directions like a horse without harness. But, instead, I knelt before him. My response was the simplest of all requests: "Lord, help me" (Matthew 15:25).

Again his answer was shocking: "It is not fair to take the children's bread and throw it to the dogs" (Matthew 15:26). If I hesitated an instant before answering, it was not because I did not understand what he meant, but because I did. I understood, all right. Proverbial sayings were a common means of conversation in our culture. I understood and I was stunned. Jews had often called us "dogs." That was their usual byword for us gentiles. But I had not expected to hear that from Jesus' lips.

Again, all kinds of retorts flashed up in my mind. My tongue was aflame with anger and sarcasm. You're just another of those superior Jews who think that God exists to do you favors. I smothered the fire and took a different approach.

What made me do it? I am not sure. Perhaps it was my deep despair over my daughter. As long as there was one drop of hope, I was willing to keep dipping in the well. But more than that, I sensed that Jesus was not just another Jewish snob. Something in his eyes told me he cared, even when his words seemed heartless.

So I persevered: "Yes, Lord, yet even the dogs eat the crumbs that fall from their master's table" (Matthew 15:27).

With these words everything changed. His sternness seemed to break. A spark of a smile warmed his face. The tone of his voice turned reassuring: "O woman, great is your faith! Be it done for you as you desire." (Matthew 15:28.)

What an answer! A compliment and a promise woven together. I sprang to my feet, said a brief but heartfelt "thank you," clutched at my skirt to keep from tripping and ran for home.

Hoping against hope, I rushed into my house. There was my daughter lying quietly on the bed. Healed. The demon gone. For the first time in months she could move normally and speak coherently.

My argument—Jesus called it my faith—had prevailed. Some fragments of bread from the Master's table had been shared with the pet dogs. Grace which was destined to go first to the house of Israel had brought rescue to a gentile home.

Jesus had proved *reasonable* after all. My arguments had reached him. My needs had moved him. My persistence had brought my answer.

I have often pondered Jesus' silence and his stubborn resistance to my plea. Was it to test my faith that he withheld an answer for so long? Perhaps. If one is to resist the temptations of life in a pagan land where idolatry and immorality are everyday occurrences, faith has to be strong.

Was it to teach his disciples lessons in persistence that he delayed his response? Possibly. Later, I heard that he had talked about importunity and patience in prayer in some of his parables. But at the time his purpose escaped me.

Were other lessons involved? Lessons of priority and purpose in his mission? He could not be everywhere at once. His mission was restricted in its scope. As Son of David he was sent to minister to David's people first, and so were his disciples. This he clearly taught them.

But he used my argument and my experience to teach them something else. God has enough grace to be shared with all people. And eventually men and women all over the world will sit at God's table and eat of God's bread. I was one of the first.

When the cool evening winds blow in from the Great Sea and refresh our hot shores, my daughter and I often walk together. We talk about God's silence—why he does not always speak when and what we want him to. I urge my daughter to be patient. "Be reasonable in your requests. Persist," I tell her, "and God will be reasonable in his response. He will do his best in his time. And that's good enough for me."

CHAPTER 6

The Centurion
Whose Servant Was Ill

The COMPASSION of Jesus

After he had ended all his sayings in the hearing of the people he entered Capernaum. Now a centurion had a slave who was dear to him, who was sick and at the point of death. When he heard of Jesus, he sent to him elders of the Jews, asking him to come and heal his slave. And when they came to Jesus, they besought him earnestly, saying, "He is worthy to have you do this for him, for he loves our nation, and he built us our synagogue." And Jesus went with them. When he was not far from the house, the centurion sent friends to him, saying to him, "Lord, do not trouble yourself, for I am not worthy to have you come under my roof; therefore I did not presume to come to you. But say the word, and let my servant be healed. For I am a man set under authority, with soldiers under me: and I say to one, 'Go,' and he goes; and to another, 'Come,' and he comes; and to my slave, 'Do this,' and he does it." When Jesus heard this he marveled at him, and turned and said to the multitude that followed him, "I tell you, not even in Israel have I found such faith." And when those who had been sent returned to the house, they found the slave well. (Luke 7:1–10.)

H IS NAME became the center of more and more conversations. As the officer in charge of the Roman guard at Capernaum, it was my duty to look into such matters. Wherever power and popularity combined, revolt was a possibility. And preventing revolt was my business. I was a centurion, captain of a hundred men.

Like scores of other centurions stationed in foreign countries from Syria to Spain, and from Africa to England, my job was to keep the Pax Romana. My troops and I saw ourselves not so much as agents of war but as emissaries of peace. In a world seething with racial, tribal and social tension, we were like lids on the pot to keep it from boiling over.

In Capernaum, for instance, my most difficult assignment was to keep various Jewish factions from hurting one another. Some were loyal to Herod, the king who ruled as Caesar's representative; some were pledged to overthrow him and to fight for Jewish independence. Local politics were not my concern unless the Roman peace was threatened. My primary assignment was to preserve it.

I had other tasks as well. Protecting the tax collectors and seeing that their revenue was delivered safely to Caesarea was one of them. I always enjoyed the trip to Caesarea. It was our link to the outside world, our gateway to Rome, the city to which all roads led. With its mighty breakwaters, its lavish palace, its huge amphitheater and its massive temple, Caesarea was a metropolis worth visiting. Walking its broad streets with the distinguished government officials or standing in its marketplace amid the merchandise of a dozen countries, one sensed something of the power and splendor of Rome. One felt a direct part of that network of government and trade which bound our world together in a tighter, stronger net than history had yet woven.

Still, I was always glad to return to Capernaum where my main responsibilities lay, responsibilities like investigating those reports about this man Jesus. I had no choice but to look into the matter because Capernaum, the city for whose order and security I was responsible, had become the hub of his activities.

My close contacts with the Jewish leaders kept me well informed of Jesus' movements. The more information I picked up, the less worried I was. He was no cheap demagogue haranguing people to foolish violence. He was no political opportunist judging the crowd's direction and racing to keep ahead of it.

As report after report came to my attention, I spent less time in concern over the possible dangers that his power and popularity might produce and more time and interest in the amazing wonders that he worked. My soldiers and I talked to many people who had been healed. That man whom Jesus cleansed of an unclean spirit on his first sabbath in Caper-

naum was well known to us. We had witnessed the seizures
to which he was prone. Now he was done with all of that,
and the whole town knew it.

You may wonder about my close contacts with the Jews
of Capernaum. After all, I was an outsider to their religion,
tongue and culture. More than that, I was an officer in an
enemy army, part of a force that for a hundred years had
occupied the land. We had been here ever since the bold
and ambitious general, Pompey, conquered Syria. The official
reason for our coming to Phoenicia and Palestine was to curb
the raids of the pirates who used the ports as havens. No
wheat ship carrying its life-sustaining cargo from Egypt to
Italy was safe as long as the pirates could find shelter in any
Mediterranean port. So we Romans came by the thousands
to make our sea safe for our ships. And we stayed—stayed to
build roads, aqueducts and temples; stayed to collect the taxes,
take the census, enforce the laws; stayed to keep the peace.

It was my role as keeper of the peace that encouraged
me to get to know the Jewish leaders of Capernaum. To
view me as a friend would make it difficult for them to harbor
secrets from me, let alone to foment open revolt. I went so
far as to help them build a new synagogue, the largest and
finest in Capernaum. Part of my inheritance I put to this use.
The Jews took great pride in it, and so did I.

The closer I got to the Jews, the more their religion
fascinated me. Caesar's current policy was religious toleration,
so long as the religion was practiced peacefully. The Jews
had freedom to worship as they would. This gave me freedom to study their religion, and I was intrigued.

There were no elaborate rituals like the ones I saw in
Caesarea. The prayers and readings were simple. No incense

offered to idols curled its way heavenward in the Jewish synagogues. The God of the Jews could not be carved in stone like the gods of ancient Rome or her modern Caesars. Even in the great temple at Jerusalem, where the feasts were celebrated and the sacrifices offered, there were no statues. Their God was too great, too powerful, too mysterious to be confined to figures of wood, metal or stone. As I heard them talk about his deeds in history—his rescue of their tribes from slavery in Egypt, his conquest of the lands they now occupied, his protection when the Assyrians and Babylonians tried to destroy their leaders and obliterate their religion, his deliverance from the vicious tyranny of Antiochus Epiphanes, the Syrian king, who had brutalized their people and desecrated their religion—I found his deeds in history were impressive, almost compelling. With increasing frequency I caught myself wondering whether they were true.

What started as a political strategy became almost a personal commitment. This was why I turned to the Jewish leaders when my servant fell ill. I had no access to Jesus. I had never met him. Usually, as was my practice, I stayed on the fringe of the crowds that teemed around him. So I asked the elders of the Jews, including Jairus, the ruler of the synagogue, to beg Jesus' help.

Nobody was closer to me than this slave of mine. Night and day he was at my elbow, caring for my personal needs, keeping my uniforms and equipment in good order, dispatching messages to my troops. He knew more about my household than I did. He was at the marketplace early in the morning to buy my food. He was at the doorway in the evening to wash my feet. And in between he performed a thousand useful chores. I not only found his services indispensable;

I enjoyed his company, admired his abilities, appreciated his fellowship.

Now he was deathly sick, gripped by a paralysis that held him tighter than any manacles a blacksmith could forge. None of my centurion's power, none of my soldierly training, equipped me to cope with this. My slave was sick of body; I was sick of heart. So I enlisted the help of my friends.

In my behalf, they argued earnestly: "He is worthy to have you do this for him, for he loves our nation, and he built us our synagogue" (Luke 7:4,5). Jesus responded immediately by starting with them on the long walk to my house. Along the shore of the lake they walked, heading south from Capernaum on the road to Magdala and Tiberias. My house was on a gentle hillside outside of Capernaum, with a sweeping view of the lake.

When my servants, who had raced ahead with the news that Jesus was coming, reached my house I was overwhelmed. I found the compassion of Jesus amazing. There was no class consciousness to it, for one thing. Who was sick? Not a ruler of the synagogue or an elder of the town, not even a Roman officer—just his slave. Yet here was Jesus, changing his plans, interrupting his schedule, diverting his course to come to my house.

Yet I knew that Jesus' compassion was not just sentimental. He was not coming because he felt he had to, but because he wanted to. Jesus' compassion was like a jewel whose setting was the refined metal of authority. I had heard the reports of his authoritative teaching. Firsthand, I had watched and admired the authority with which he handled the throngs that followed him.

Compassion for even a slave, yet the authority of a general

who could command legions—this combination of attributes prompted me to act. As Jesus and his company drew near my house, I sent some friends to him with a message: "Lord, do not trouble yourself, for I am not worthy to have you come under my roof; therefore I did not presume to come to you. But say the word, and let my servant be healed. For I am a man set under authority, with soldiers under me: and I say to one, 'Go,' and he goes; and to another, 'Come,' and he comes; and to my slave, 'Do this,' and he does it." (Luke 7:6–8.)

Eagerly and anxiously I waited for my friends to return. Would Jesus understand my message? How would he take it?

As I waited and watched at the window, I also listened to the sounds of sickness which came from the cot where my servant lay. Suddenly his moaning ceased, and I sensed the stir of movement. I ran to his side and found him sitting up. He took my hand and pulled himself to his feet. In far shorter time than I can tell it, he had been healed.

My friends rushed into the room to share my rejoicing. But the healing hardly surprised them. "We expected it," they exclaimed, "because Jesus was so impressed by your faith—a faith which he said was greater than any he had seen in Israel."

Compassion, that's all I can say. A sick slave, yet Jesus had compassion on him: no social limits to his compassion; it leaped over the barriers of class. A gentile, yet Jesus had compassion on him: no religious limits to his compassion; it hurdled the walls of religion. A Roman centurion, yet Jesus had compassion on me: no ethnic boundaries to his compassion; it vaulted the obstacle of race.

In fact, Jesus seemed to find some symbolism in what he

had done for me. My friends brought me his words, and afterward I heard the Jews discussing them with some vexation. "I tell you," Jesus affirmed, "many will come from east and west and sit at table with Abraham, Isaac, and Jacob in the kingdom of heaven, while the sons of the kingdom"—this was the part that vexed my Jewish friends—"will be thrown into the outer darkness; there men will weep and gnash their teeth" (Matthew 8:11,12).

I don't pretend to know all that Jesus meant, but I do know this: though I had been an outsider to the faith of Israel's God, I somehow felt that I now belonged. I had met the compassionate God of Abraham, Isaac and Jacob. I had met him in Jesus of Nazareth.

CHAPTER 7

Simon, the Pharisee
Who Took Jesus
to Dinner

The FORGIVENESS of Jesus

One of the Pharisees asked him to eat with him, and he went into the Pharisee's house, and sat at table. And behold, a woman of the city, who was a sinner, when she learned that he was sitting at table in the Pharisee's house, brought an alabaster flask of ointment, and standing behind him at his feet, weeping, she began to wet his feet with her tears, and wiped them with the hair of her head, and kissed his feet, and anointed them with the ointment. Now when the Pharisee who had invited him saw it, he said to himself, "If this man were a prophet, he would have known who and what sort of woman this is who is touching him, for she is a sinner." And Jesus answering said to him, "Simon, I have something to say to you." And he answered, "What is it, Teacher?" "A certain creditor had two debtors; one owed five hundred denarii, and the other fifty. When they could not pay, he forgave them both. Now which of them will love him more?" Simon answered, "The one, I suppose, to whom he forgave more." And he said to him, "You have judged rightly." Then turning toward the woman he said to Simon, "Do you see this woman? I entered your house, you gave me no water for my feet, but she has wet my feet with her tears and wiped them with her hair. You gave me no kiss, but from the time I came in she has not ceased to kiss my feet. You did not anoint my head with oil, but she has anointed my feet with ointment. Therefore I tell you, her sins, which are many, are forgiven, for she loved much; but he who is forgiven little, loves little." And he said to her, "Your sins are forgiven." Then those who were at table with him began to say among themselves, "Who is this, who even forgives sins?" And he said to the woman, "Your faith has saved you; go in peace." (Luke 7:36–50.)

I DON'T REALLY KNOW why I invited him to my home. If I were honest, I would say it was partly because I was curious and partly because I wanted to make political capital.

My curiosity was high. What kind of man was it who could capture the imagination of these crowds so that they hung on his every word as the Queen of Sheba did on King Solomon's? Was he charlatan or prophet? Was his aim to feed the people like a good shepherd or to fleece them like an impostor?

I was curious. I wanted to find out what his plans for the future were. Would he join our party and cast his lot with us Pharisees in our power struggle with the Sadducees? In all that I had heard of his teaching he did not seem to support the Sadducees and the wealthy landowners who were their leaders. He had more in common with the farmers, fishermen and artisans from whom he came. And he certainly did not seem to support the elaborate rituals of the temple, which the Sadducees made the center of their religious life.

In fact, one account reported that at the beginning of his public ministry he drove the animal vendors and the money changers out of the temple. He even talked in veiled, mysterious words about the destruction of the temple.

None of this would sit well with the Sadducees. The temple ceremonies and sacrifices, the rites and rituals of the five books of Moses, were the heart of their faith. This is where we parted company with them, we Pharisees. Certainly we revered the temple and its priesthood, but we placed a higher premium on individual obedience to the law—to all its parts, to its every detail.

That's why we studied the law so diligently. Our scribes had combed through it line by line, precept by precept. Six hundred thirteen commandments they found in the law: two hundred forty-eight commands that told us what to do; three hundred sixty-five commands that told us what not to do.

One of our tasks as Pharisees was to help the common people keep the law. Bear in mind that there were only a few thousand of us throughout the land. We were an insignificant minority in our numbers. Our significance came from our influence in the synagogues. We tried to make an impact at the grass roots. The temple? It was largely under the control of the priestly families, almost all of whom were Sadducees. The Sanhedrin, the council of seventy-one elders that controlled much of our political and religious life? It was largely made up of Sadducees, although some of our party were represented and could press for their points of view.

But the synagogue was where we were in charge. Here we taught the law. Most of the common people were either ignorant or heedless of the law. They might have adhered to its main points, the basic laws of diet and so forth, but its details escaped them.

We Pharisees were dedicated to it in totality. To us the law—the whole set of commands, statutes and ordinances in the five books of Moses, in the prophets and in the writings—was like a seamless garment. It could not be divided into more important and less important parts. To break one commandment was to break the whole law.

To help the common people keep these commandments, we built hedges around the individual commandments. That is, our scribes and rabbis in the four hundred years since Ezra's day, when the law was restored to our people after their long decades of captivity in Babylon, developed specific interpretations of each commandment. The sabbath commandment, for instance, forbade work on that holy day. What was work? When did the sabbath begin and end? What kinds of emergencies did we recognize, emergencies wherein work was legitimate? If an ox fell into a hole in a field on the sabbath, could we put ropes around him and pull him out without breaking the commandment?

It was our concern for the common people and their need to know the law that raised my curiosity about Jesus to a peak. We made it a practice to keep a watchful eye on spiritual leaders or religious teachers who came along, especially those who proved popular with "the people of the land," which is what we called the common people.

And it certainly would not hurt my standing with these people to have Jesus in my home. In popularity he was miles ahead of any Pharisee I knew. Political capital with the people was what we needed. I felt I could gain a good bit, personally and for our party, by offering hospitality to Jesus.

Not that I went all out in my gestures of friendliness. We were rushed. The crowds that flocked after Jesus had detained us, making it past the dinner hour when we reached my door. I dispensed with the normal acts of hospitality because of the lateness of the hour. I did not even wash Jesus' feet, as I normally would have done for a guest. We merely washed our hands—a ceremonial act which we Pharisees always practiced before meals—and then we reclined to eat.

I must confess, though, that more than the lateness of the day was involved in my meager show of hospitality. I was uncertain as to how I should treat Jesus. The whole experience had me on edge. One part of me said, "Have nothing to do with this man; he's dangerous." Another side said, "This is the most impressive figure to come on the scene since the great prophets like Amos, Isaiah, Jeremiah." I argued with myself. Should I invite Jesus or shouldn't I? *Should* won the argument, but my indecision made me shy away from the cordial acts of hospitality which I would otherwise have performed.

You can imagine how shocked I was when that woman of seamy reputation slipped into my house and flooded Jesus with her acts of devotion and hospitality. Our houses were usually open to the street. Anybody could walk into the courtyard and see what was going on through the open doors or windows. So in she had come and she had brought an alabaster flask of ointment with her.

She stood behind Jesus, by his feet which were extended over the end of the couch where we were reclining to eat. She was weeping—for the joy, I suppose, of being in his presence.

She began to wet his feet with her tears and to wipe them with the hair of her head. Then she bent over to cover his feet with kisses and finally to anoint them with her valuable ointment.

In stunned surprise I watched the scene, watched especially for Jesus' reaction. Would he be tempted by the charms of the woman? Would he try to fondle her or make a silent appointment to meet her later? Did he know what kind of woman she was? Her reputation in the community made her an outcast. No synagogue would welcome her. No adherent of the law would even greet her in the street. In fact we usually crossed the road to avoid any contact, and looked away so as not to defile our eyes and minds by reflection upon her lewdness.

Yet Jesus let her touch him. Why? What kind of prophet was he? If he did not know about her, he was not truly a prophet. If he did know about her and received her this way, he was not a worthy representative of our law and customs.

Jesus broke the silence by addressing himself not to her but to me: "Simon, I have something to say to you." "What is it, Teacher?" I answered. Then he embarked on a story that seemed to steer the conversation on an irrelevant course: "A certain creditor had two debtors; one owed five hundred denarii, and the other fifty. When they could not pay, he forgave them both. Now which of them will love him more?"

To a Pharisee, learned in the logic of the law, the answer was simple: "The one, I suppose, to whom he forgave more." And while I was still puzzling over the purpose of his question, Jesus turned toward the woman and said to me: "Do you see this woman? I entered your house, you gave me no water for my feet, but she has wet my feet with her tears and wiped them with her hair. You gave me no kiss, but from the time I came in she has not ceased to kiss my feet. You did not anoint my head with oil, but she has anointed my feet with ointment. Therefore I tell you, her sins, which are many, are forgiven, for she loved much; but he who is forgiven little, loves little." (Luke 7:44–47.)

Like a hot coal dropped in my lap, Jesus' point hit me and burned me. As Nathan the prophet had trapped King David with the parable about the rich man who stole the poor man's sheep, so Jesus used a parable to snare me.

The point of the parable was the contrast between that woman, with her open reputation for sin, and me, a Pharisee, a man separated unto the law of God, a man of devotion and conviction. She had shown great love for Jesus; I had shown little. I, his host, had skipped the customary acts of hospitality; she, a stranger, had lavished her attention upon him.

My thoughts were a swirl of confusion. I was hurt; I was anxious; I was resentful; I was perplexed; I was envious. This woman had intruded on our privacy and interrupted our conversation. I resented her, and yet I could not help but envy her.

She was of the streets, yet she seemed to understand Jesus better than I. I was a student of the law, but she seemed to have tasted true faith. I had developed some theories about Jesus' powerful appeal to people, but she had felt that power firsthand and responded to it.

Perhaps what confused me most were Jesus' final words to her: "Your sins are forgiven. . . . Your faith has saved you;

go in peace." (Luke 7:48,50.) I felt the outrage of my friends, who were offended by this brash display of divine authority, this superhuman presumptuousness: "Who is this, who even forgives sins?" (Luke 7:49).

Yet I had another feeling. Why did Jesus not grant the same gift—the gift of forgiveness—to me, his host, a Pharisee? Perhaps it was because I had not asked.

CHAPTER 8

Zacchaeus,
the Tax Collector
Who Turned Honest

The SALVATION of Jesus

He entered Jericho and was passing through. And there was a man named Zacchaeus; he was a chief tax collector, and rich. And he sought to see who Jesus was, but could not, on account of the crowd, because he was small of stature. So he ran on ahead and climbed up into a sycamore tree to see him, for he was to pass that way. And when Jesus came to the place, he looked up and said to him, "Zacchaeus, make haste and come down; for I must stay at your house today." So he made haste and came down, and received him joyfully. And when they saw it they all murmured, "He has gone in to be the guest of a man who is a sinner." And Zacchaeus stood and said to the Lord, "Behold, Lord, the half of my goods I give to the poor; and if I have defrauded any one of anything, I restore it fourfold." And Jesus said to him, "Today salvation has come to this house, since he also is a son of Abraham. For the Son of man came to seek and to save the lost." (Luke 19:1–10.)

I HAD HEARD that one of his disciples had been a tax collector. That was enough to arouse my curiosity when I learned that Jesus was to pass through Jericho.

I had not met Matthew—Levi, I think they used to call him—until then. But his story was well known to me. As chief of the tax collectors of the region around Jericho, I had access to news from both Galilee and Judea. For a prominent religious leader like Jesus, a man whom the people considered a prophet, to receive a tax collector, a publican, into his company was news that traveled far and fast.

Ordinarily the opposite was true: men of my profession were rejected by the religious leaders, shunned as though our bodies were spotted with leprosy. In their eyes we were more than just unpopular; we were unclean.

Most of the citizens of the land despised us. And not without reason. We worked for the Romans, who for a century or so had occupied the land. And we had the distasteful job of collecting taxes from the residents in the area and exact-

81

ing customs duty from the foreign merchants who passed
through.

On top of this, we often taxed at exorbitant rates or placed
unfair values on the merchandise. Fraudulence was our standard practice.

Our regular contacts with Roman officials and other gentiles with whom we had to do business meant that we were
unclean in the sight of the devout Jews, especially the Pharisees. Barred from synagogue and temple by this supposed
contamination, we were forced to form our friendships and
build our social relationships outside the religious community.
Any spark of religious hankering we might have had, any
flicker of spiritual curiosity, was bound to be quenched by
the utter rejection we felt from the religious community.

Our needs were no concern of theirs. Their devotion to the
letter of the law built an insuperable wall between us and
them. The Sadducees were not quite so bad. Realists that
they were, they had accepted the fact of Roman occupation,
with its political obligations like taxes. They adjusted themselves to our presence and, in the main, were civil if cool
toward us.

But the Pharisees were another breed. They not only
shunned us themselves, but they prodded the people to make
life hard for us. Woe to any citizen who dealt kindly with a
publican, who talked with him in the marketplace, who
invited him as guest to table. All the righteous wrath of
those spiritual separatists would descend on his head. It
would be like Judgment Day come early when the Pharisees
got through with him. "Publicans and sinners" was a household phrase. The two terms were almost synonymous.

That's what had made Jesus such an object of curiosity among us. He had taken one of our company into his. Most Jewish leaders would not even say "*shalom*" to us on the street, yet he had taken one of us into the heart of his group. The Pharisees would not eat anything we had touched, yet he ate every day from a common dish with Matthew. The Pharisees would not stand near us in the market or at the city gate, but Matthew, a tax collector, slept by Jesus' side night after night.

I had mused on this for months, as reports came to Jericho from Galilee in the north. Then a fascinating story raised my curiosity even higher. It seems that Jesus had come into open controversy with the Pharisees. The differences between him and them grew sharper. More and more they began to attack him for his claim to be the Son of God and for his disregard of their strict interpretations of the sabbath laws. And more and more he began to expose their hypocrisy, the meticulous way they kept the details of the law while they shattered its spirit.

The story that fascinated me was one of his parables which he told frequently to make his teaching clear and pointed. It seems that two men went to the temple in Jerusalem to pray. One was a Pharisee; the other, a publican. That's what made the story important to me. The message of Jesus' parable lay in the differences between the prayers of the two men.

The Pharisee stood aloof from the other worshipers in pride and self-righteousness. On the surface his prayer was a poem of thanksgiving, but at the heart it was an announcement of self-worth. He thanked God that he was not like other men, especially like the publican who was praying by himself in a corner of the temple courtyard. The Pharisee reminded God that he had obediently kept his fast every Monday and Thursday and had always paid his tithe on anything that came into his hands.

The publican's prayer was different. Even his posture showed this. Too humble to raise his head and hands in prayer, he bowed his head and smote his chest. His act of contrition reminded me of the way the Jews mourn on their Day of Atonement. But this was no special holiday, just an ordinary time for prayer. Yet this was no ordinary prayer. The publican begged God for mercy. He called himself a sinner, not just a sinner in the sense that the Jews called him a sinner because he violated some of their rituals, but a sinner who had failed God, who had not measured up to his standards of worship and love, who had no bargaining power and no claim to favor.

Yet in the story Jesus told, this man—this wretched outcast tax collector, this practitioner of our despised profession —went away justified. I could hardly believe my ears as friends told me the story. A publican justified! That was a change! Rejected, hated, cast out, deplored, abused—these were the terms to describe a publican. But Jesus said the man was justified. He had begged for mercy and got it. He had simply asked. And received.

You can understand now my eagerness to see Jesus as he passed through Jericho. Jericho had been my home for a number of years. Working there was the best assignment I had ever had in my years of service to Rome. The weather was warm without being unbearable, and the winters were wonderfully mild. A generation or so earlier Herod the Great had lived there and spent lavish sums of money not only on his own palaces but on the town itself—its walls and fortifications, its theater and amphitheater.

To be chief publican there was a responsible and lucrative assignment. Jericho and its environs were among the most fertile areas in Palestine. Figs and sycamores and palms grew in abundance. Especially important were the balsam plantations. When the winds were right the balsam fragrance was wafted for miles to the surrounding towns. The balsam trees were valuable for perfume, and a chief source of my income was the tax exacted from the noblemen who owned these plantations.

Jericho's situation also made it an advantageous place for my kind of work. Almost every caravan from Damascus in the north or the Arabian desert in the south had to pass through there. It was at the main junction to Jerusalem, and, indeed, to all of Judea. Caravans of spices and precious woods, caravans of fine cloth and valuable jewels, passed through regularly. From them all I exacted tribute for Caesar and a living for myself.

The procession that captured the attention of the citizens of Jericho that day, however, was not the swaying line of camels from Arabia, not the firm-footed gray donkeys of Damascus; it was a parade of pilgrims from the north, from Galilee. And at their head was Jesus. Spirits in Jericho were high. The streets were lined with men, women and children who cheered the pilgrims and stood on tiptoes to see the prophet of Nazareth.

The crowd was too much for me. I hated crowds like this. For one thing the people often seized the opportunity to push and pummel and even spit on me. They could get away with it in the enthusiasm and facelessness of a crowd. Also I am short of stature. That's hard to admit, and I almost choke as I say it. But I'm small, and crowds make it difficult for me to see.

That day in Jericho I threw my pride to the warm winds that swept down from the hills of Moab, and I climbed a tree. Nothing could stop me from seeing Jesus. So the rich and infamous chief tax collector of Jericho climbed a tree along the route where Jesus was bound to pass.

The cheers of the throng grew louder. As the procession and its mysterious leader drew near my tree, the noise was almost deafening. Then the procession halted right beneath me. I almost fell in surprise. Jesus looked up and with a gesture that was half invitation and half command, he shouted: "Zacchaeus, make haste and come down; for I must stay at your house today" (Luke 19:5).

The reports about Jesus were true. The parable that I had heard was a reality. The prophet of Nazareth would have fellowship with a publican.

My unbounded joy was matched by the dark disapproval of the citizenry, especially the priestly family. A dozen of the best homes in town would have opened to Jesus, had he so much as hinted. But he came to stay with me.

All that I was and was not came into focus in conversation with him. He knew my needs before I could recite them. He read my heart without a word from me.

That conversation was too personal, too intimate, too precious, to be repeated here. It is enough to say that my life was so radically changed by Jesus' love for me, his acceptance of me and the forgiveness that I felt, that I resolved to make amends as best I could for the wrongs I had worked, the hurt I had caused. "Behold, Lord," I promised Jesus, "the half of my goods I give to the poor; and if I have defrauded any one of anything, I restore it fourfold" (Luke 19:8).

Jesus' answer was the best news I had ever heard. A word of praise from the proconsul who managed the affairs of Rome on these distant shores, a citation from Herod or a letter of commendation from Caesar himself would be like idle gossip in comparison. "Today salvation has come to this house, since he also is a son of Abraham. For the Son of man came to seek and to save the lost." (Luke 19:9,10.)

Salvation, with its freedom and its wholeness, was mine in that moment. The guilt of my crimes and the rejection by my countrymen were behind me. I now belonged to God. I, who had been barred from my religion by my occupation, was truly in faith as well as by blood a son of Abraham.

Much more could be said. But deeds, not words, are my chief concern. The poor need caring for. My wrongs I must set right. I am a son of Abraham, a son of God; I must get on with the tasks of this sonship.

CHAPTER 9

Bartimaeus,
the Blind Man
Who Begged for Mercy

The MERCY of Jesus

And they came to Jericho; and as he was leaving Jericho with his disciples and a great multitude, Bartimaeus, a blind beggar, the son of Timaeus, was sitting by the roadside. And when he heard that it was Jesus of Nazareth, he began to cry out and say, "Jesus, Son of David, have mercy on me!" And many rebuked him, telling him to be silent; but he cried out all the more, "Son of David, have mercy on me!" And Jesus stopped and said, "Call him." And they called the blind man, saying to him, "Take heart; rise, he is calling you." And throwing off his mantle he sprang up and came to Jesus. And Jesus said to him, "What do you want me to do for you?" And the blind man said to him, "Master, let me receive my sight." And Jesus said to him, "Go your way; your faith has made you well." And immediately he received his sight and followed him on the way. (Mark 10:46–52.)

I T WAS the high season of the year for those of us who begged for a living. Passover was at hand, the most important of our Jewish feasts, and the roads were jammed with pilgrims on their way to Jerusalem.

Jericho was both a junction point and a resting place for these travelers. Almost everyone coming from the east or the north passed through our town. The best roads from Galilee lay on the east of Jordan. The normal route led the pilgrims south of the Lake of Galilee, across the Jordan near the point where it emptied out of the lake, and then down the east bank. Where the sharp turns of the gorge and its steep banks made traveling difficult, the road went a good way east through less rugged terrain.

A couple of hours' walk from Jericho the pilgrims crossed the river again and prepared for the sharp, dangerous, uphill climb to Jerusalem. The journey up the hill to the sacred city took only about six hours. But the pilgrims usually spent the night in Jericho and then got an early start to avoid the heat and the thieves. No one wanted to be on that road after sundown. The jagged stone cliffs, with dark shadows that concealed caves and crannies, made the canyon through which the road passed a den of robbers. Almost every week there were reports of beatings and plundering. No wary traveler made the journey by himself. The risk was too great.

The Passover pilgrims began to arrive a week or more before the great feast. They had relatives in Jerusalem and its neighbor towns. Passover meant family reunions. There were ceremonies of purification to undergo in the temple, special sacrifices to offer, holy vows to keep. Passover meant religious devotion.

The pilgrims were cheerful as they anticipated spending time with relatives. The pilgrims were thoughtful as they reflected on their conduct, their obedience to the law, their concern for the poor.

It was a good time for begging. Feelings of compassion ran warm. Devotion to duty dug deep. Almsgiving was one of the results. Those of us on the receiving end always looked forward to this season. Pilgrims meant alms, alms far above what the regular residents of Jericho could give. Not that they were all stingy. Some of them gave regularly and generously at their synagogues. Each synagogue had a box for coins and a plate on which food could be placed. These gifts kept those of us who could not work alive during the year. And then came Passover with its opportunity to get ahead a little, to live a notch or two above mere survival.

I was ready for Passover. Every day at dawn one of my relatives would lead me to the edge of town, the western edge. There I would sit, calling to the travelers—calling for mercy, begging for alms. A joyous lot they were, heady with hopes for the Passover, eager to catch the first glimpse of David's splendid city, to gaze at the sparkling sun as it was reflected on the columns of the temple.

As they walked, they sang. They sang the psalms of David, psalms written for pilgrims:

> "On the holy mount stands the city he founded;
>   the LORD loves the gates of Zion
>   more than all the dwelling places of Jacob.
> Glorious things are spoken of you, O city of God."
>
> (Psalm 87:1–3.)

And they also sang:

> "Those who trust in the LORD are like Mount Zion,
>   which cannot be moved, but abides for ever.
> As the mountains are round about Jerusalem,
>   so the LORD is round about his people,
>   from this time forth and for evermore."
>
> (Psalm 125:1,2.)

As they sang, I used to cry out with the loud, strident voice that years of use had produced. Sharp and clear, it pierced the air like the howl of a jackal on a winter's night. And they heard me and threw their alms—a couple of coins, a loaf of bread, a piece of fruit.

I never knew who gave what. The jumble of voices, the clap of sandals on the dusty road and the click of donkeys' hooves were what I heard. I could not see the color and pageantry of the processions and the light on eager faces. I was blind; I had been from birth.

Touch, taste, sound, smell—these senses I had. But I was

condemned to use them in total darkness. I would have traded any two of them to see the almond blossoms in the spring, to watch the cattle roam the hills of Moab, to know my mother's face. Dark and dependent was my world. Wherever I went, others led me. Whatever I did, others helped me with. My hands could not earn a living without eyes to guide their work. My feet could not journey far from home without sight to direct their paths.

But Passover was on the way. And that provided some distraction at least, and a bit of extra income. Then things took an extraordinary turn. I could hear a commotion that seemed to come from the center of Jericho. No one around me knew what it was at first. As the shouts grew louder, reports came our way that Jesus of Nazareth had entered the city and was going to spend the night at the home of Zacchaeus, chief of the tax collectors of Jericho.

Him I knew. Even beggars were not exempt from his cruel policies. Any of us who had a handful of coins had to pay off the men of Zacchaeus. Roman soldiers would harry us to the point of torture if we didn't.

At first I was incensed. Was this prophet from Nazareth actually going to eat and drink and sleep with the most fiercely loathed man in Jericho? How could this good and noble teacher, this wise man and healer, this descendant of King David, keep company with a traitor?

Then I thought again. Did I dare take hope from Jesus' stay with Zacchaeus? Was there a chance that a prophet who could be kind to a publican would also heal a beggar?

Zacchaeus and I were not altogether different, although the Lord knows how I disliked him. Rejection was a way of life with both of us. Outcasts we were: he through his profession; I through my infirmity. Good people avoided the company of both of us: his because he was unclean; mine because I was cursed. He was defiled by his gentile contacts and his handling of untithed moneys; I was accursed by the sin that had brought my blindness. *Whose* sin I did not know. But sin there must have been to account for my condition. That's what I had always been told.

Jesus had spent the night with Zacchaeus; perhaps he would have a moment in the morning for me. Those were my thoughts as I rose before dawn and set out with my guide for my customary spot outside of town. I wanted to be there when Jesus passed by.

I sat down and waited. The pilgrims who had risen earliest began to trickle by. Some of them gave me alms. Then what seemed to be a tumult began to come within hearing. Could this be Jesus? I hardly dared wish. I feared that it might be, and he would ignore my plea. I hoped that it would be, and he would come to my aid. As the crowd drew nearer, the bystanders and other beggars around me caught a glimpse of the man from Nazareth and told me it was he.

By now the noise was deafening, especially to my ears, which were sharpened to a keen edge of sensitivity by decades of diligent listening. Loudly, almost raucously, I began to call: "Jesus, Son of David, have mercy on me!" Harshly, yes cruelly, the people who stood in front of me, between me and Jesus' procession, turned and told me to be quiet. Only they put it in blunter language than that.

But I was determined. The years of darkness had made me desperate. I tried to push my silencers away, while I cried louder than I ever had in my life. It was now or never. Another few steps and Jesus would have been beyond my reach. My

voice would have been lost in the tumult as the procession
trudged up the hill. The pilgrim song would have drowned my
plea.

All my hope of healing and all my despair of blindness
combined to produce a shout the like of which Jericho had
seldom heard. Partly the howl of a wolf and partly the roar
of a lion, it came: "Son of David, have mercy on me!" I
could hear the parade halt suddenly. Then one voice rose
above the throng. "Call him," the voice commanded. It was
Jesus, and he was calling me.

The people who had tried to shut me up came to my aid.
"Take heart; rise, he is calling you," they hollered as they
pulled me to my feet. Like a buck in spring I leaped to my
feet and hurried toward the sound of Jesus' voice. My hands
groped their way through the crowd until I stood before him.

His words were what I had hoped to hear: "What do you
want me to do for you?" My answer took no thought. I begged
for no alms. I asked for no spiritual instruction. Relief from
my problem, *the* problem, was what I wanted. The words
poured out: "Master, let me receive my sight." Jesus responded to my cry for mercy. He did not test, taunt, tease.
He did not raise any questions or exact any pledges. He
spoke, and his speech was charged with action: "Go your way;
your faith has made you well."

Faster than I can tell it, my eyes were opened. Light, color,
faces and forms flooded my mind. The experience was over-
whelming, almost intoxicating. "Hallelujah! Hallelujah! Hallelujah!" was all I could say.

The procession moved on, and I did not return to my spot
beside the road. I no longer begged alms from the Passover

pilgrims. Instead, I joined them, more eager than they for a look at Jerusalem.

Talk about a feast. More than my stomach, it was my eyes that feasted. Those first impressions have never left me. I can still see them as I tell my story. I have seen Jerusalem many times since then, but that first visit is what I remember.

Even more I remember the face of Jesus, the first sight that met my eyes. There was total darkness; then suddenly I saw his face.

Amid the din of the Passover throng he heard my plea for mercy. And his answer was the light of his own face. What mercy, what love, what grace!

CHAPTER 10

Joseph,
the Man Who Lent
Jesus His Tomb

The KINGDOM of Jesus

Now there was a man named Joseph from the Jewish town of Arimathea. He was a member of the council, a good and righteous man, who had not consented to their purpose and deed, and he was looking for the kingdom of God. This man went to Pilate and asked for the body of Jesus. Then he took it down and wrapped it in a linen shroud, and laid him in a rock-hewn tomb, where no one had ever yet been laid. It was the day of Preparation, and the sabbath was beginning. (Luke 23:50–54.)

I WOULD BE hard pressed to say when I first came to believe in him. I do know that I certainly had come to trust him fully as my Lord and Messiah the night I tried to save his life.

It was a terrifying responsibility to be a member of the Sanhedrin, the highest Jewish court in the land. There were seventy-one of us on the council that made the major decisions on religious, moral and even political issues. So great was our power and so ancient our traditions that the Romans rarely interfered with our work, though they did reserve the right to intervene when Caesar's key policies were at stake.

Capital punishment, for instance, was a decision that we could not make on our own. The Roman procurator, as our governor was called, had to confirm any death sentence we issued. This is why the trial of Jesus went through so many stages: before the high priests; before Pontius Pilate, who was the Roman procurator; and before Herod the King.

Jesus' trial was the worst night of my life, and the worst meeting of the Sanhedrin I had ever sat through. Not that it was a regular meeting. It was hastily called by Caiaphas, high priest at the time and our presiding officer. Only the members who lived in or near Jerusalem were summoned to attend, and I protested this when it happened. So did Nicodemus. But our pleas fell on the ears of our colleagues like seeds on stony ground.

Their animosity against Jesus had reached fever pitch. They were so frightened by his power, so baffled by his wisdom and threatened by his influence, that death was the only solution that would satisfy them. In the long history of our council, which in a sense reached back to the seventy elders who helped Moses administer the affairs of the twelve tribes, there had never been a decision so scandalous as this.

We and our forebears had wrestled with delicate issues frequently. During four of the past five centuries we had been an occupied land. During the time of Ezra when the Sanhedrin first became active as the chief council, the Persians were our captors. After them came Alexander and his Syrian successors, like the cruel and wicked ruler Antiochus Epiphanes. We had no prophets in those days to bring God's word, so the Sanhedrin had to interpret the law as best it could. For a century or so we gained our freedom and drove the pagan conquerors from our hills and valleys. We tried to cleanse the land of heathenism and live in obedience to our laws and customs as a God-fearing people. Then came the Romans. Some of what they brought was good. Their architects and engineers laid strong, straight roads and built graceful aqueducts. But I always considered the Roman presence among us as a compromise. Their government was reasonably efficient, but efficiency was no substitute for freedom. And their paganism and mythology I had no stomach for. My commitment was to the God of Abraham, Isaac, Jacob—to his law, to his promises, to his kingdom. Anything else was at worst a scourge, at best an inconvenience.

The Sanhedrin was not really free to do God's will for his people as long as we had to reckon on the Romans. However, we cannot blame that long night of sham trial on the Romans. Reason had fled like a rabbit before a jackal. And our leader, Caiaphas, was as much to blame as anyone.

Our customary procedures were ignored; our usual dignity turned to panic. Ordinarily we sat in a semicircle for our trials. Two clerks sat with us: one to record the votes for acquittal, the other to record the votes for condemnation. The accused person was on hand to hear the deliberations and to testify in his own behalf.

We took our responsibilities with full seriousness and did all that we could to protect the rights of innocent persons. A simple majority vote was all that we needed to acquit a man, but it took two out of every three votes to condemn him. When the time came to vote, roll was called and each member stood to register his vote. The youngest members voted first, because we wanted them to make up their own minds without the pressure of knowing what their elders had decided.

All this, I say, was normal procedure, the way we usually carried on our business. But this particular night was not normal. Blood ran hot. The frustration that had seethed within our officials for months reached the boiling point and spilled over. I was chagrined; I was anxious; I was angry; I was ashamed. And, worst of all, I was helpless.

The high priest was beside himself, and the members were out of hand. This august body had become a mob gone mad. This solemn court surrounded its prey like ravening wolves.

The picture became all too clear: corruption, utter corruption, was in command. The court of law had turned into a conspiracy of death.

At the head of it were the old priests. Annas, who had been high priest fifteen or so years before, was part of the plot. He had apparently questioned Jesus earlier, trying to trick him into condemning himself with some blasphemous claim. Now Annas reported how insubordinate Jesus was, and how he refused to answer the old priest's questions.

Then Caiaphas, our presiding officer, called for witnesses. Most of those who came forward said nothing to incriminate Jesus. Finally, a couple of men stood up and mumbled something about Jesus' boast that he could destroy the temple and build another one in three days. This was the straw that Caiaphas was waiting for, and he clutched it for all he was worth. He tried to force Jesus to acknowledge openly that he was the Messiah, the Son of God.

Jesus' answer had the ring of the words of the prophet Daniel: "You have said so," he told Caiaphas. "But I tell you, hereafter you will see the Son of man seated at the right hand of Power, and coming on the clouds of heaven." (Matthew 26:64.)

At that point Caiaphas exploded. Jesus had identified himself with Daniel's "Son of man," who was to bring the final victory to our people. The high priest tore his clothes and shrieked at us in the Sanhedrin: "He has uttered blasphemy. Why do we still need witnesses? You have now heard his blasphemy. What is your judgment?" (Matthew 26: 65,66.)

Almost to a man, my colleagues answered, "He deserves death." I was stunned. My friends and associates—the wealthy Sadducees, leaders of the priestly families; the scrupulous

Pharisees, with their allegiance to the law in all its points; the elders, distinguished heads of the great families of the land; the retired high priests; the scribes, learned in the words of Moses—all of them were thirsty for his death. Like vultures they pounced on the occasion and cried for blood. No roll call, no counting of a quorum, no waiting till the next day to announce the decision. Death was their verdict, and I knew they would have their way.

The rest was formality. Pilate had no taste for controversy. The last thing he needed was to enter into pitched battle with the leaders of the people. Herod would not intervene. Political capital was to be gained by going along with the decision, not by resisting it. And political capital was the staff of life to Herod.

It was the lowest moment of my life. Until that death-dealing decision was made, I had scarcely realized how much vested interest I had come to have in Jesus. Suddenly, terribly, finally, I thought my hopes for God's kingdom had come to an end.

Not many of my countrymen took the hopeful promises of the prophets with full seriousness. They were jaded, discouraged by centuries of foreign domination. They were either absorbed in their meticulous devotion to the law like the Pharisees, preoccupied with political opportunism like the Sadducees, or consumed with the struggle to keep food in their stomachs and a roof over their heads. Almost no one had time or nerve to hope for God's kingdom. But I did.

When John the Baptist stormed through the land, calling in that stern, deep voice of his, "Repent, for the kingdom of heaven is at hand," I was among the few who began to sense what he meant. Then when he told us that he was not God's

Messiah but just a voice sent to prepare his way, I began to take an interest in Jesus of Nazareth, to whom even John paid allegiance.

I followed the reports of his ministry with keen attention as they filtered down from Galilee. At the high holidays I made it a point to listen to him when he made the pilgrimage to Jerusalem and preached or answered questions in the market-place or temple courtyard. Nicodemus, my friend and colleague in the Sanhedrin, noted my interest and confided in me that he too was deeply impressed by the Nazarene. Once he shared with me a secret conversation that Jesus and he had had one night—a conversation that changed Nicodemus' life and gave him spiritual power and insight beyond anything he had ever known.

We had never supported Jesus openly, Nicodemus or I. Fear of losing face may have been part of the reason. But part of it too was our hope that by remaining in the background we might more effectively influence our leaders in his behalf than if our support were a matter of public knowledge.

Now all that had failed. Jesus had been led away to the last stages of his hollow trial. My hopes that he would bring God's kingdom, that he would be David's son and heir, that the government would be upon his shoulders, lay broken on the Sanhedrin floor. They had been shattered by the stammerings of false witnesses, crushed by the hatred of Annas and the treachery of Caiaphas.

No kingdom there. I was dejected and remained so throughout the night. The next day I stood sadly among the crowd that watched the tragic story reach its doleful end on a cross.

I had failed to speak publicly for Jesus; I had failed to persuade my associates not to condemn him. All I could do now was to offer the use of my new tomb, which stood in a garden not far from the place of crucifixion. Though my home was in Arimathea, a little way to the north, I had chosen to be buried in Jerusalem, where I had lived throughout most of my career.

Pilate could not turn me down when I asked for permission to bury Jesus. He only wanted to make sure Jesus was actually dead, and then he released the body to me. I bought the best linen shroud I could find in the market, wrapped Jesus in it and laid him in the tomb. With a huge stone which rolled in a trough before the doorway I sealed the door. And with that burial and that seal, I laid to rest all my hopes that Jesus would bring the kingdom I had yearned for.

Then came Sunday morning. My linen shroud was laid aside. My huge hewn stone was rolled from the door. My fine new tomb was empty once again. The kingdom has come. And Jesus is the King.

CHAPTER 11

Mary Magdalene, the Woman Who Served Jesus to the End

The LORDSHIP of Jesus

And also some women who had been healed of evil spirits and infirmities: Mary, called Magdalene, from whom seven demons had gone out ... (Luke 8:2).

Now on the first day of the week Mary Magdalene came to the tomb early, while it was still dark, and saw that the stone had been taken away from the tomb. So she ran, and went to Simon Peter and the other disciple, the one whom Jesus loved, and said to them, "They have taken the Lord out of the tomb, and we do not know where they have laid him." Peter then came out with the other disciple, and they went toward the tomb. They both ran, but the other disciple outran Peter and reached the tomb first; and stooping to look in, he saw the linen cloths lying there, but he did not go in. Then Simon Peter came, following him, and he went into the tomb; he saw the linen cloths lying, and the napkin, which had been on his head, not lying with the linen cloths but rolled up in a place by itself. Then the other disciple, who reached the tomb first, also went in, and he saw and believed; for as yet they did not know the scripture, that he must rise from the dead. Then the disciples went back to their homes.

But Mary stood weeping outside the tomb, and as she wept she stooped to look into the tomb; and she saw two angels in white, sitting where the body of Jesus had lain, one at the head and one at the feet. They said to her, "Woman, why are you weeping?" She said to them, "Because they have taken away my Lord, and I do not know where they have laid him." Saying this, she turned round and saw Jesus standing, but she did not know that it was Jesus. Jesus said to her, "Woman, why are you weeping? Whom do you seek?" Supposing him to be the gardener, she said to him, "Sir, if you have carried him away, tell me where you have laid him, and I will take him away." Jesus said to her, "Mary." She turned and said to him in Hebrew, "Rab-boni!" (which means Teacher). Jesus said to her, "Do not hold me, for I have not yet ascended to the Father; but go to my brethren and say to them, I am ascending to my Father and your Father, to my God and your God." Mary Magdalene went and said to the disciples, "I have seen the Lord"; and she told them that he had said these things to her. (John 20:1–18.)

I T WAS NOT until some time later that I understood what he meant. I wanted to hold on to him, to cling to him. But he would not let me. We thought we had lost him forever on that dark afternoon when the sun refused to shine. Now here he was alive, speaking, calling me by name—not the gardener as I had thought at first, when I could barely make out his features in the dawn's dim light; but my Lord, my Master, risen from the dead.

Instinctively, compulsively, I rushed to him and flung my arms around him. I wanted to hold on to him as if my life depended on it. As a drowning woman would clutch the body of her rescuer, I wanted to hang on to him.

He was back from the dead, and I was filled with a sudden rush of hope—hope that our life together would continue as it had been those many months. Almost like a family we had traveled together through the cities and villages of Galilee—Jesus, his twelve disciples, and a number of women, especially my friends Joanna and Susanna. Like a family we traveled—eating together, praying together, listening to Jesus as he brought the good news of the kingdom of God to the huge throngs that gathered wherever he went. We discussed these deep mysteries with him privately, when the crowds had dispersed and a handful of his closest followers remained to tend to his needs and to be strengthened by his company.

Those were great days. And as I heard him call me by name in the garden on that cool morning at the beginning of the week, I dreamed that those days would continue. That's why I wanted to hold on to him.

There was no way that I could put into words what he meant to me. Language is incapable of explaining what he had done for my life. "Transformed" is too weak a word to describe the change he had worked in me.

My past was so grim, my memories of it so haunting, I have no desire to rehearse its sorry details. All my adult life I had been beside myself, out of control, thoroughly disturbed. My life was like a loosely woven garment. It was constantly unraveling, and the unraveled strands were continually tangled. I was a wreck. Like the battered hull of a boat beaten against the rocks on the shore of Galilee, I was tossed and pummeled by the forces of life until I was senseless.

Then Jesus came. Seven demons he had to cast out. I had been completely possessed. They had seized and occupied my mind and body as pirates commandeered the Roman ships that carried grain from Egypt. Then, at his word, they were gone.

I had my life back again. Its tangled threads were rewoven into an orderly, attractive pattern. The battering storms had ceased, and I could sail a straight course. The vicious pirates had been driven from their command. Jesus became Master of my life.

My only thought from that day on was to follow him. And follow him I did through those golden days in Galilee. Teeming crowds, mighty miracles, dynamic preaching—these were the context of my new life.

As the opposition of the Pharisees mounted and Jesus' popularity seemed to wane, I followed him. More and more he spoke of suffering and death. He seemed to have a premonition that his time was short, that his life was pressing toward a deadly climax. His "hour," he called that climax. Those of us who followed him were frightened by the growing opposition and baffled by the veiled but dire predictions that Jesus made. Yet we continued to follow him.

We followed him to Jerusalem on that last momentous journey. I was with him in Jericho when he brought the news of salvation to Zacchaeus, the chief tax collector. I was part of the procession that halted for a few minutes on the edge of Jericho when Bartimaeus, the blind beggar, cried for mercy.

Up the long hill from Jericho to Jerusalem I followed Jesus. With tears of joy in my eyes, I watched the crowds acclaim him as the Son of David with strong shouts of "Hosanna! Blessed is he who comes in the name of the Lord."

Later that week my weeping was for sorrow, as word came that Jesus had been arrested in the Garden of Gethsemane. In stunned, almost incredible silence, I stood with Jesus' mother and a few of our friends and watched the life drain out of his body. His voice was barely audible as he entrusted John with the care of Mary, his mother.

He, whose whole person had been so charged with power, was helpless. Wracked with pain were those hands and arms whose touch had brought healing to the multitudes. The whole scene left me limp and faint. The darkness of the cruci-

fixion afternoon soon blended with the darkness with which
the sabbath began. In the fleeting moments between the time
when he gained Pilate's permission to bury Jesus' body and
the beginning of the sabbath, when all work had to cease,
Joseph of Arimathea, with his friend Nicodemus, had hastily
wrapped Jesus' body and placed it in his own unused tomb.
Proper preparation with spices was impossible on that hurried
afternoon, although Nicodemus had brought an abundant
supply. Joseph sealed the doorway to the tomb with a flat
stone, which sat on edge before the opening, forming a crude
but effective door.

The sabbath began, probably the worst I had ever spent. A
few of us women who had known so much joy and excitement
together huddled in Jerusalem. We could hardly talk. Periodi-
cally we broke into loud cries of lament. At other times we
wept quietly. The future we faced was as dark as the inside of
Joseph's sealed tomb. That sabbath seemed endless.

You can imagine, then, how I felt when I heard him call
my name in that familiar accent, that gentle voice. You can
see why my first thought was to hang on to him. You can
see why I did not understand it when he told me I was not to
cling to him. This was my Lord. He had set me free, brought
order to my life, given purpose and meaning to my every day.
This Lord of mine had been taken, and now he had returned.
Of course I wanted to cling to him.

The sabbath ended at sundown. While it was still dark I
went to the garden tomb with a couple of friends. We wanted
to make sure that the body was properly prepared for burial.
When I got close enough to see, I had the surprise of my life:
the huge flat stone had been taken away from the door of the

tomb. In the dim light I could barely make out the dark opening and the gray stone, which had been rolled to the side.

My first thought was to run for help. Peter and John were the ones I turned to. Breathlessly I told them about the stone and the unsealed tomb. Before I could finish they ran for the garden, John racing ahead of Peter. When I reached the tomb behind them they were clear inside, looking at the empty, slablike shelf where Jesus' body had been. There was no body, only the linen cloths with which Joseph had done the wrapping, and the napkin which he had placed on Jesus' head.

Those last few fateful days had meant blow after blow to those of us who loved Jesus. But this was more than I could take. Deprived of his leadership by his crucifixion, I was now robbed of the slight comfort I could gain by taking proper care of his body. The tragic nightmare could not even be brought to a quiet conclusion. The body was gone.

Peter and John wanted me to return home with them. I could not. Stunned into numbness, I stood weeping outside the empty tomb. Almost refusing to accept the unbelievable turn of events, I peered inside once again. This time I saw not an empty slab but two angels.

They asked me why I was weeping. As I struggled for breath to answer them, I was aware that someone had slipped up behind me. I turned as the unknown figure asked the same question the angels had: "Woman, why are you weeping? Whom do you seek?" In the dim light, my eyes full of tears, I thought it was the gardener. "Sir, if you have carried him away, tell me where you have laid him, and I will take him away." I could not even face him as I spoke.

Then I heard my name. I recognized his voice and tried

to cling to him. That was when he spoke the puzzling words that only later did I come to understand: "Do not hold me, for I have not yet ascended to the Father; but go to my brethren and say to them, I am ascending to my Father and your Father, to my God and your God."

Of course I had to obey. This was my Lord speaking. Since the bright day when he sent those demons fleeing, his lordship had been my chief concern. Now he seemed to be even more the Sovereign. He had defeated death with the same lordly ease that had evicted the spirits that were first tenants and then landlords of my mind and body.

As the weeks went by I came to understand what Jesus meant by "ascending to the Father." His lordship took on another dimension. No longer would he walk and teach among us. He was going to the Father, to that place of power and glory which was reserved for him at the Father's right hand.

I was not to hold on to him because his whole relationship with his followers was to change. Mighty works *we* were to do, because he went to the Father. His Spirit would give us wisdom and power; his church would provide our encouragement and fellowship.

His relationship with the Father was different from ours. This is why he said, "I am ascending to my Father and to your Father, to my God and your God." He was God's Son from all eternity. For this reason he could truly be Lord. I became God's child on that great day when Jesus spoke his words of rescue to me.

For a while he had come to live among us, then to die and to rise again. "Don't hold on," he had said. "I have other work to do with God my Father. You have your work to do here for your God and Father."

His words began to sink in. The full meaning of his Lordship I began to grasp. His mission was to be carried on in heaven, at the Father's side. My mission was to be carried out on earth, in the Spirit's power. I could not hold on to him. His mission here was fulfilled. Mine had just begun.

Conclusion

Eleven persons—a fraction of a vast host—have told their stories. But from them we have learned more than enough to respond to Jesus.

We have been confronted with his authority, consideration, power and confidence in their experiences. We now know more than enough to begin to trust him in all our circumstances.

His reasonableness, compassion and forgiveness shine through every episode. We now see more than enough reason to give him all our love.

His salvation and mercy flood each scene. We now can bathe in those waters and find more than enough healing for our souls' diseases.

His kingdom and lordship trumpet their glory from every

page. From their certain sounds we now hear notes more than clear enough to spark our hopes for the future.

Eleven people return to witness to the Savior, eleven men and women whose stories have gained a powerful hearing in every century and on every continent. They have brought the fullness of Christ to us by sharing the good news that turned their lives around. Thanks to the living Book in which they speak, the living church to whom they speak, the living Spirit through whom they speak, we have met Jesus too.